super

FISHING

Jason Page

Illustrated by Tony Kerins
Consultant: Mike Ashpole

Endorsed by The National Junior Anglers
Association

Hodder
Children's
Books

a division of Hodder Headline

Text copyright 1998 © Jason Page
Illustrations copyright 1998 © Tony Kerins
Published by Hodder Children's Books 1998

Edited by Jacqueline Dineen
Designed by Fiona Webb
Series designed by Fiona Webb

10 9 8 7 6 5 4 3 2 1

A catalogue record for this book is available from the British Library.

ISBN: 0 340 791675

Printed by Clays Ltd, St Ives plc

Hodder Children's Books
a division of Hodder Headline
338 Euston Road
London NW1 3BH

Meet the author

Jason Page has been fishing for 22 years and writing children's books for seven. He has won awards for his writing but sadly not a single trophy for angling. On the other hand, he has eaten a number of the fish he has caught but has yet to eat one of the books he has written. This book (uneaten) is dedicated to Colin, with love.

Acknowledgement

Special thanks to Mike Ashpole of Ashpoles of Islington for answering all my questions. You've displayed the patience all young anglers need!

Introduction

People think sitting by the river bank fishing must be boring. In fact, for sheer excitement nothing can beat that heart-stopping moment when you see your float disappear and you realise you've got a bite. But fishing is not just about catching fish. That's why its called fishing, not catching! Learning how to fish is all about trying to understand the ways of a wild creature. Fishing brings you really close to nature in a way that few other hobbies do.

This book is designed to get you started on fishing. Hopefully, you'll get hooked!

Jason

Contents

Gone fishing

super.activ
FISHING!

Congratulations – you've just landed your first great catch. This book!

Whether you want to fish in lakes, canals, rivers or even the sea, this book will show you how. It's got all you need to know about fishing – or rather, it's got all you need to know about angling, which is what most fishermen (or anglers!) prefer to call their hobby.

It's a fact!

There are no less than three million anglers in the UK. That makes angling the most popular sport that people actually do (rather than just sit and watch) in the whole country!

Angling techniques

With this book, you'll be able to master the three most popular angling techniques: float fishing, ledgering and spinning.

Float fishing ▼

A float sits on the surface of the water with your baited hook dangling below. When a fish nibbles the bait, the float moves – so you know you've got a bite!

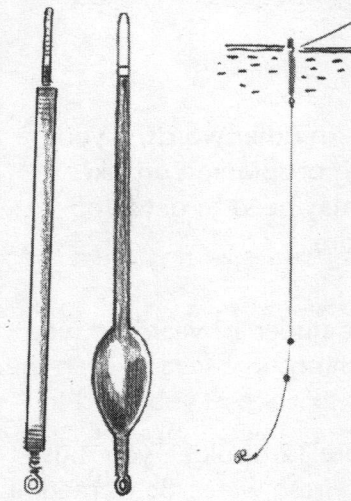

Spinning ▲

A spinner is a type of lure that looks like a little fish as you pull it through the water. Spinners are used to catch predators, such as zander, that eat other fish.

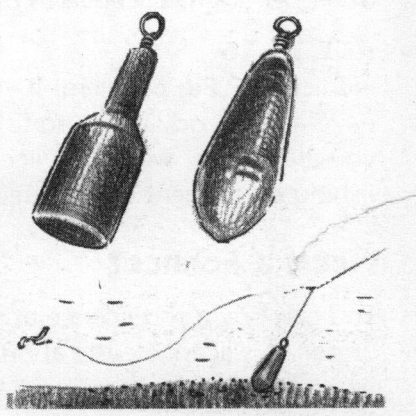

Ledgering ▶

A ledger is a weight that carries your baited hook down to the bottom. Unlike a float, a ledger won't get moved around by the water or the wind.

Coarse fishing

You can use floats, ledgers or spinners on any type of water to catch all sorts of fish. On fresh water (water that isn't salty), this type of fishing is known as coarse fishing. And there are certain rules and regulations that everyone who goes coarse fishing must obey!

Rod licence

If you want to go coarse fishing – in other words, if you want to go float fishing, ledgering or spinning on lakes, canals, rivers or reservoirs – you may need to get a rod licence. It depends how old you are.

UNDER 12

No licence? No problem! If you're under 12 years old, you don't need a rod licence to go fishing.

AGE 12–16

No licence? Big problem! If you are 12 or older, you must have a valid rod licence to fish on fresh water. Be warned, if you are caught without a licence, you may have all your fishing equipment confiscated.

Need a licence?

You can buy a rod licence at your local post office. An under-16's licence costs about half the price of a CD and lasts for a whole year.

Fishing permit

You can't simply go coarse fishing anywhere you like. You must get permission! If you are lucky, a friendly farmer might allow you to fish in his lake for free. But in most cases, you will have to buy a fishing permit.

A fishing permit is a ticket that allows you to go fishing somewhere. Some permits are just for one day and are pocket-money prices. Others last for up to a year and are more expensive. What's on offer varies from place to place.

The best way to find out about fishing permits where you live is to talk to the people who run your local tackle shop. They will know where you can go fishing, what sort of permit you need and where you can get it. In most cases, you can buy a permit on the day from a bailiff who walks along the bank.

NO FISHING Without Permission!

Record collection

The oldest fishing club in the world is the Ellen Fishing Club in Scotland. It was formed more than 150 years ago, in 1829.

Closed season

The final rule to remember about coarse fishing is that there is a closed season. During this period, you cannot go fishing on rivers or streams. Fishing also stops on some lakes and canals, although others stay open all year round. The closed season lasts for just three months, from 15 March to 15 June. This rests the banks and allows the waterbirds to nest. It also gives the fish a chance to breed without being disturbed by anglers!

DON'T FORGET
You can still go fishing on some lakes and canals during the closed season. Ask your local tackle shop or fishing club about fishing spots near you that stay open all year.

Record collection

The largest fish ever caught using a rod and line was a great white shark. The fierce man-eater weighed over 1,200 kg and measured more than 5 m from tip to tail! It was caught off the coast of South Australia in 1959.

Sea fishing

Coarse fishing isn't the only way to catch fish using floats, ledgers and spinners. Similar tackle and techniques are also used to catch fish that live in salt water.

Three good things about sea fishing.

No licence

You don't need a rod licence to go sea fishing, no matter how old you are!

No permit

You can go sea fishing off most harbour walls, jetties, piers and beaches without having to buy a permit. If there isn't a sign that says you can't go fishing, then you can!

No closed season

There is no closed season for sea fishing. You can fish all along the coast the whole year round.

One not-so-good thing about sea fishing.

No sea!

Not everyone lives near the sea. This means some people can only go sea fishing on holiday. On the other hand, everybody lives somewhere near a lake or a reservoir, a river or a canal, so coarse fishing is something anyone can do.

Be warned!

Don't use coarse fishing tackle to go sea fishing. The salt water will damage it! Have a look at the specialist sea fishing gear on pages 24-5

11

Safety first

No matter what sort of fishing you want to do, the basic rules about safety are the same. The best advice is always to go fishing with a friend. That way, if one of you gets into trouble, the other one can fetch help. And if the fish decide to ignore you, at least you'll have someone to talk to!

- Learn to swim. If you are not a good swimmer, don't go fishing on your own. The better you are at swimming, the safer you will be. But, even if you are a strong swimmer, never be tempted to go for a quick dip in fishing waters. You could get tangled in discarded line or hurt yourself on old hooks and tackle.

- Always tell someone where you are going and what time you will be home. Once you have made arrangements, stick to them! Don't leave the area where you said you would be just because the fishing isn't as good as you hoped. And don't stay late just because the fish are in a feeding frenzy.

- Always check the weather forecast before you go fishing. Angling in a thunderstorm isn't just pointless, it's dangerous! Make sure you take the right clothes with you (see page 14) and be prepared for the unexpected. Nothing ruins a day's fishing like being drenched in a downpour or getting sunburnt.

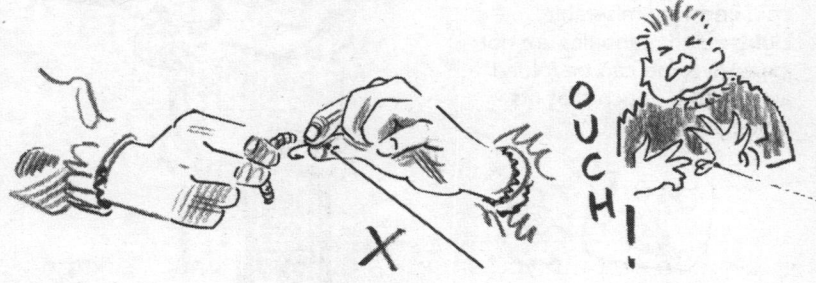

- Be careful with fishing equipment. Hooks are for catching fish, not fingers! When you are holding a hook that's attached to a line, always make sure that the line is slack. If the line is taut and your rod gets knocked, the hook will be pulled into your finger. Ouch!

- Learn how to handle fish correctly (see page 102). Some species, such as pike, have sharp teeth and can give you a nasty bite. Others, such as perch, have pointed spines that can pierce your skin. If you don't know what you are doing, you could injure yourself as well as hurting the fish.

What to wear

Fishing is a great excuse for wearing your worst clothes. You need gear that is warm and comfy. Bear in mind that you may end up sitting for hours on a muddy river bank so choose clothes that you don't mind getting dirty.

Hat with a brim
A hat with a peak or wide brim is always a good idea. In cold weather, it helps to keep your head warm. When the Sun is out, the brim helps to shade your eyes and protects you from sunburn.

Waterproof
A waterproof is essential, even when the weather forecast says it won't rain. An unexpected shower can leave you drenched, cold and very miserable. Light-weight cagoules are not expensive and can be folded away into a pouch that fits inside your pocket.

In your pocket – a phone card
Always carry a phone card or enough change to call home.

On your feet
Wear shoes with good grips on their soles. Old trainers are fine for fishing along the banks of a canal or on a pier but Wellington boots are better where it's likely to be muddy – along rivers, streams and lakes, for example.

Sunglasses with Polaroid lenses
On a bright day, a pair of shades is a must, for two reasons. The glare of the Sun reflecting off the water can give you a rotten headache. It also stops you seeing the fish moving around below the surface. But make sure your sunglasses have Polaroid lenses. These cut out the reflected light, protecting your eyes and allowing you to see through the water.

In your pocket – sun cream
Sun cream for sunny days is another essential item. Remember, the Sun's rays don't have to feel hot to burn you. Choose a cream with a protection factor of at least 10.

Lots of layers
Several layers of clothing are much better than one big, thick jumper. They keep out the cold more effectively, and it's also easy to peel off a layer or two if you start to feel too hot.

Fingerless gloves
Fingerless gloves keep your hands warm but leave the tips of your fingers free to do fiddly jobs such as tying knots. You can buy them in most sports shops but they are easy to make. Just cut the fingertips off an old pair of gloves.

Long trousers
Avoid wearing shorts. Your legs can get badly sunburned in summer and you may need to climb over brambles and walk through stinging nettles to get to a good fishing spot.

What else do you need to go fishing?

Fishing tackle, of course! And that's what we'll be dealing with in the next chapter.

2 Tackle this – the basics

Before you can go fishing, you're going to need a bit of basic tackle. Specialist gear can be expensive but you should be able to buy everything you need to start fishing for the same price as just five CDs.

Rods

Some rods are designed exclusively for just one type of fishing but if you want to try a bit of everything, go for a 10-ft* rod, which is long enough for float fishing but short enough to go spinning with. Make sure that it has a screw end (take a look at the picture on page 17) so you can do some ledgering too.

*Fishing rods are still measured in the old-fashioned Imperial units called 'feet' rather than the modern metric units known as 'metres': 3 feet is about the same as 1 metre.

Can you handle it?

The handle on a coarse fishing rod should stick out about 5 cm beyond your elbow (see below). If the handle is too long, the rod will be difficult to control, especially when casting. If it is too short, your wrist will soon get tired during a fight with a big fish.

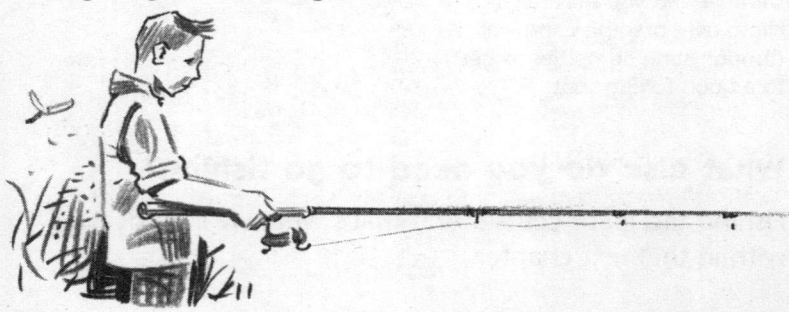

Some rods have a screw end. This allows you to attach a swing tip or quiver tip (see page 60) to the rod for ledgering.

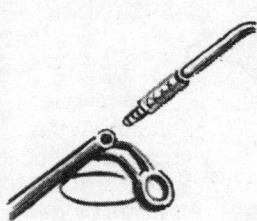

Most float-fishing rods are made of three separate pieces. Spinning and ledgering rods usually come in two parts.

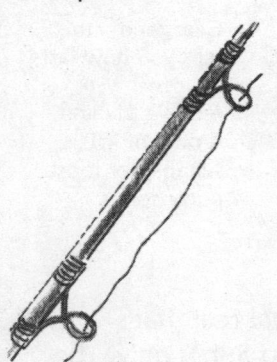

The fishing line is threaded along the rod through rings called eyes.

Modern rods are made of carbon and glass fibre. This makes them strong but very light.

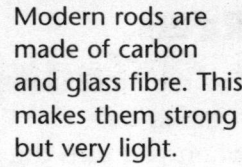

Two rings on the handle fit over the bottom of the reel and hold it firmly in place. On most float and ledger rods, these rings slide all the way along the handle so you can adjust the position of the reel. On spinning rods, they are usually fixed.

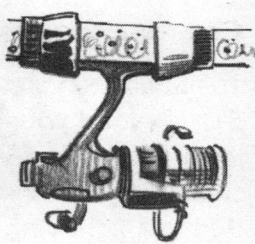

Lots of rods have cork handles. Cork gives a good grip, feels warm in winter and is easy to replace when it gets worn.

Reels

The most popular type of reel is the fixed-spool reel. It has a rotating bale arm that winds the line around the spool when you turn the handle. This type of reel can release a lot of line very quickly, so you can cast long distances.

Fixed-spool reel

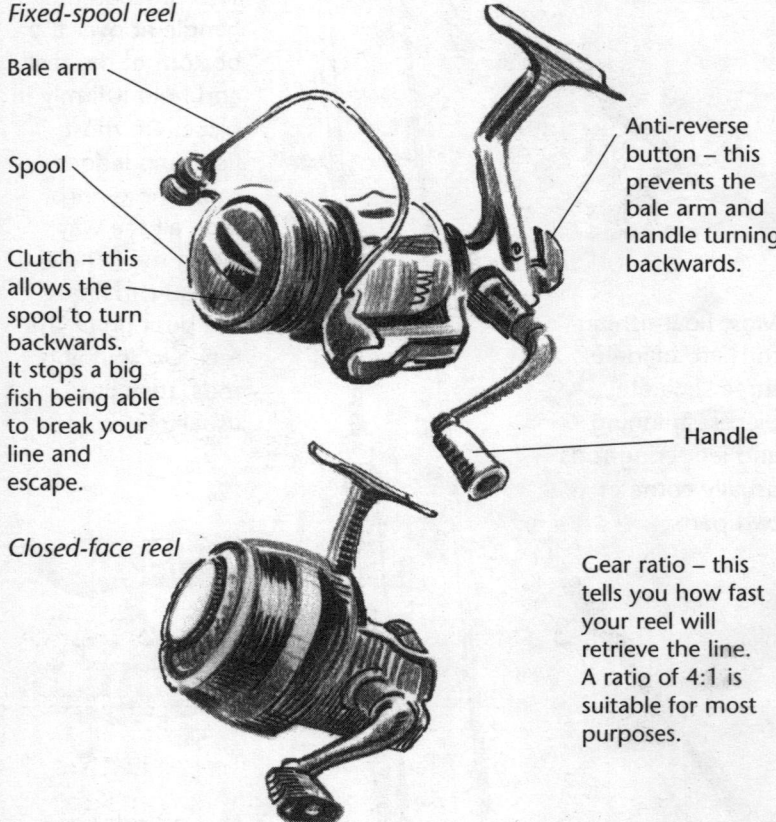

Bale arm

Spool

Clutch – this allows the spool to turn backwards. It stops a big fish being able to break your line and escape.

Anti-reverse button – this prevents the bale arm and handle turning backwards.

Handle

Closed-face reel

Gear ratio – this tells you how fast your reel will retrieve the line. A ratio of 4:1 is suitable for most purposes.

The closed-face reel is a kind of fixed-spool reel that's designed for use with light lines (less than 5 lb*) only. The spool is enclosed in a case which stops the wind blowing line off the spool.

* Another Imperial unit – pounds (lb) – is used for fishing lines: 1 lb is about 450 g.

Loading a spool

Use a double slip knot to tie the end of the line around the spool. Then get someone else to hold the line, keeping it tight, while you turn the reel and wind it on.

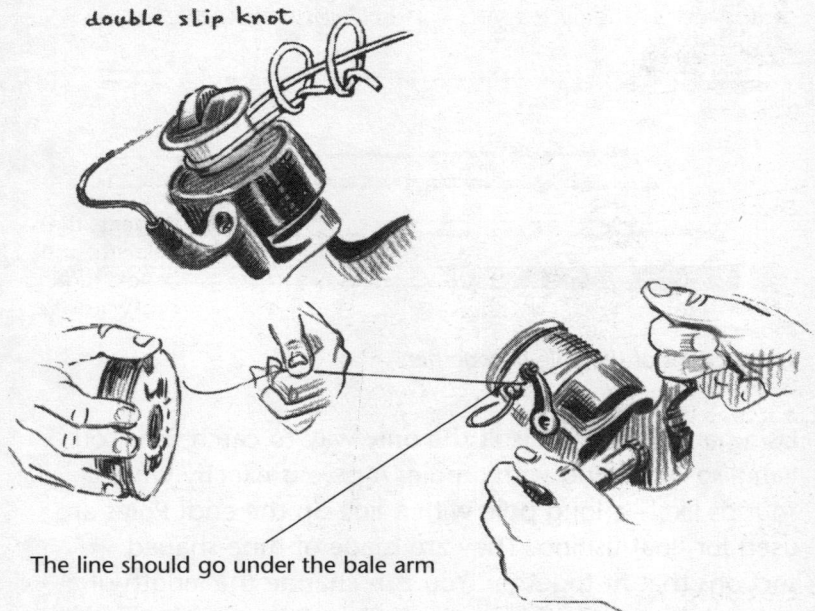

double slip knot

The line should go under the bale arm

DO YOU KNOW?

How much line you should put on a spool? See for yourself on page 27.

DON'T FORGET

If you're fishing with a fixed-spool reel, make sure that when the bale arm is closed the line goes underneath it. Otherwise, when you turn the handle nothing will happen!

Reels for left-handers

Most reels can be adjusted to suit left-handed anglers. You simply unscrew the handle and attach it to the other side.

Poles

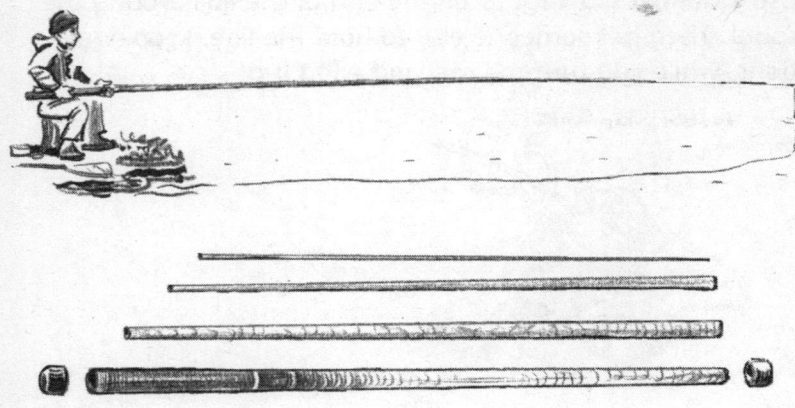

The sections of the pole fit together.

Using a rod and reel isn't the only way to catch fish. You can also go fishing with a pole. A pole is exactly what it sounds like – a long pole with a line on the end! Poles are used for float fishing. They are made of tube-shaped sections that fit together. You can change the length of a pole while you are fishing simply by adding or removing a couple of sections.

When is a pole not a pole?

The answer is – when it's a whip! On a pole, the line is attached to a piece of elastic inside the end sections. If the line is simply fixed to the end of the pole, the pole is known as a whip.

The longest poles can measure up to 16 m from end to end! But there's no need to go to such extraordinary lengths. An 8 m pole is easily long enough and half that length will do for a whip.

How does a pole work?

You don't use a reel on a pole. The line is attached to a piece of elastic that is stretched inside the last section or the last two sections of the pole. When you get a fish on the end of the line, the elastic stretches. This allows you to play the fish.

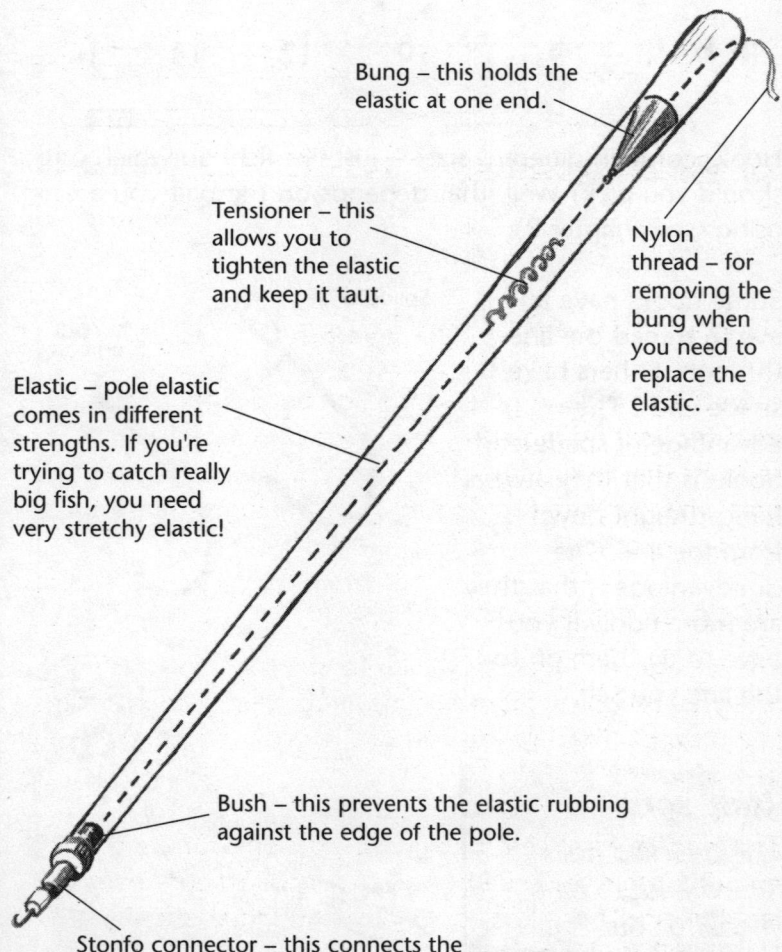

Bung – this holds the elastic at one end.

Tensioner – this allows you to tighten the elastic and keep it taut.

Nylon thread – for removing the bung when you need to replace the elastic.

Elastic – pole elastic comes in different strengths. If you're trying to catch really big fish, you need very stretchy elastic!

Bush – this prevents the elastic rubbing against the edge of the pole.

Stonfo connector – this connects the elastic to the fishing line.

21

Hooks and lines

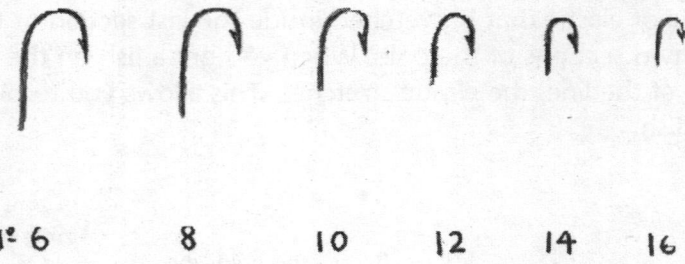

Nº 6   8   10   12   14   16

Hooks come in different sizes – just like fish! So which one should you pick? Well, that depends on the bait you are using (see chapter 9).

Some hooks have an eye to thread the line through. Others have spade ends. The advantage of spade-end hooks is that they always hang straight down from the line. The disadvantage is that they are more fiddly if you have to tie them on to the line yourself.

Spade end

Eyed end

Knot spot

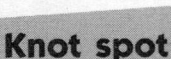

Use a locked half blood knot to tie a hook to your line.

Hooks come in different shapes as well as different sizes. A crystal bend hook is ideal for fishing with maggots. A round hook is better when you are using worms for bait.

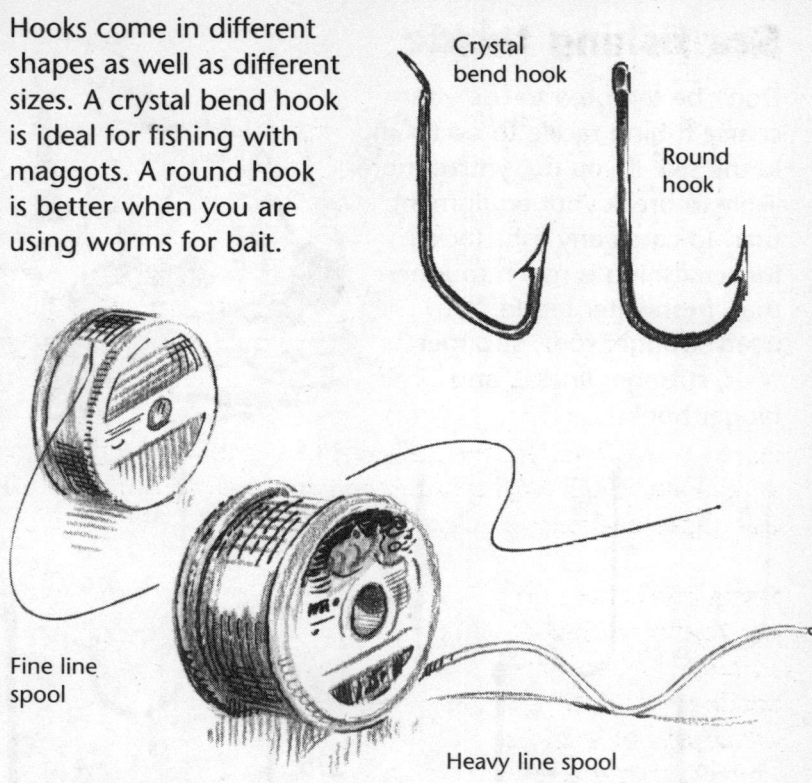

Crystal bend hook

Round hook

Fine line spool

Heavy line spool

The most popular type of fishing line is made from nylon and is called monofilament (or mono for short). Lines come in different strengths, known as breaking strains. Like choosing which hook to use, your choice of line depends on the fish you are trying to catch and how you are trying to catch them. You'll find out more in chapters 5, 6 and 7. Just remember that heavy lines may be stronger but they are also more likely to be noticed by the fish.

Record collection

A 130-lb (59-kg) line was used to catch the biggest ever fish caught on a rod, a 5-m man-eating great white shark (see page 10). That's some line!

Sea fishing tackle

Don't be tempted to use your coarse fishing tackle to go fishing in the sea. If you do, you're more likely to break your equipment than to catch any fish. Tackle for sea fishing is much tougher than freshwater tackle. You need stronger rods, stronger reels, stronger lines… and bigger hooks!

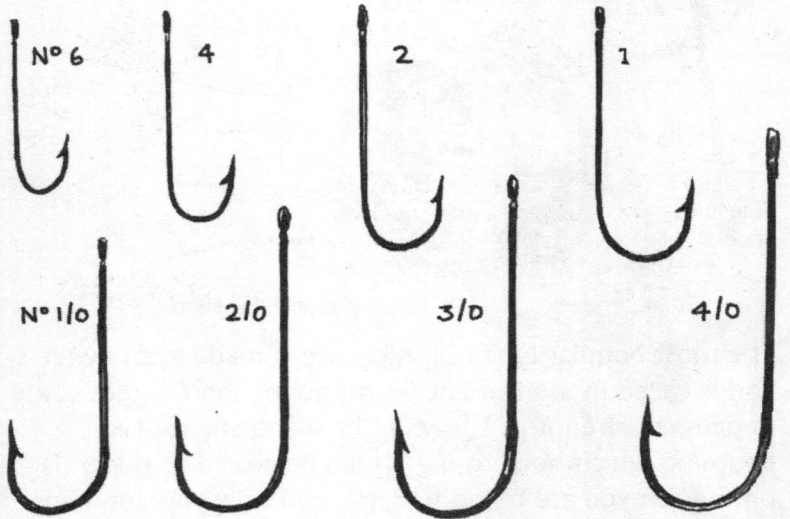

N° 6   4   2   1

N° 1/0   2/0   3/0   4/0

Sea fishing hooks are larger and stronger than coarse fishing hooks. They are also given a protective coating to stop them rusting in salt water.

Remember, if you don't want to buy your own sea fishing gear, you can sometimes hire what you need in tackle shops near the coast.

An 8-ft rod is long enough for fishing off a pier but if you want to fish off the beach, you'll need a 12-ft beachcaster. The handle on this type of rod should be longer than on a coarse rod. This is because you need two hands to cast (see page 27).

Beachcasters are about the same size as float fishing rods but they are much stronger.

Metal parts are coated to prevent saltwater corrosion.

Beachcasters are made of two pieces.

Sea rods have larger eyes than coarse fishing rods.

Grip for right hand.

The fixed-spool reel is also the most popular type of reel for sea fishing.

Grip for left hand.

Record breaker

It's possible to cast very long distances using a beachcaster. The record currently stands at 257 m. Reckon you can do better than that? Then you'd better start reading chapter 3.

3 Casting off

Being able to cast effectively is one crucial skill you must master. It's no use spending your hard-earned cash on fancy floats and slick spinners if all you do is hurl them into the bushes.

Oh well, maybe I'll catch a flying fish!

Casting is the art of getting the bait to land exactly where you want it. If you can crack casting, you're well on the way to a full keep-net. But before you reach for your rod and line, cast your eyes over these safety tips.

Safety first

- Never cast near an overhead cable. If your line or rod touch a power line you will get a shock that can kill.
- Before each cast, always check that no passers-by are in the way. If your rod hits someone, you could cause a serious injury.

Getting ready to cast

Before you can cast, you must adjust your reel to release
the line. If you don't, no line will come off the reel and you
won't cast very far at all! However, before you do this, you
must trap the line with your finger. This will stop the weight
of your terminal tackle pulling line off the spool before you
have cast.

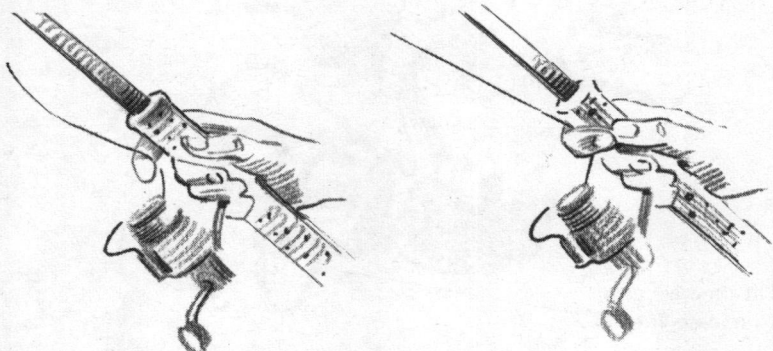

*Hook the tip of the first finger on your right hand over the line then
press it firmly against the rod. (If you're left handed, follow the same
instructions but use your left hand when the instructions tell you to
use your right and vice versa.)*

Tackle tip

*On a fixed-spool reel, the line should fill the spool to just
below the rim. A spool that isn't full increases drag on
the line, reducing the power of your cast.*

Casting off

With the line trapped securely against the rod, use your other hand to adjust the reel so that line will come off the spool when you cast. How you do this depends on the type of reel you are using.

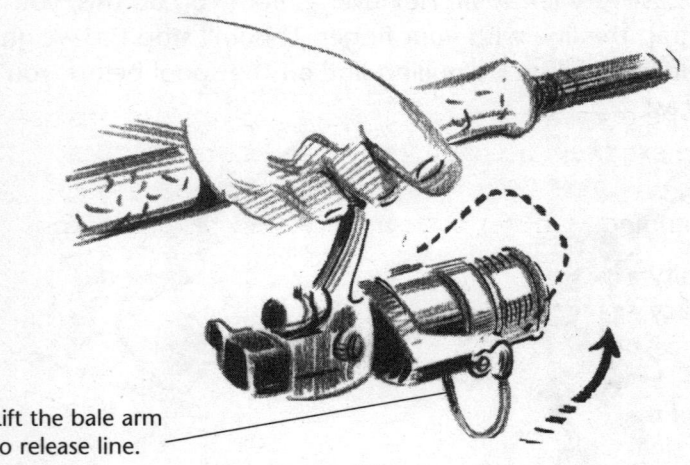

Lift the bale arm to release line.

Fixed-spool reels have a bale arm which stops line coming off the reel. Before you cast using this type of reel, you must lift the bale arm up.

Some closed-face reels have a line release button which you must press to release the line. On other models, you need to push the front of the reel with your finger.

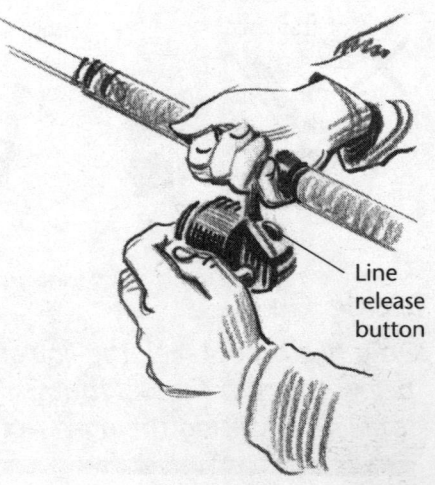

Line release button

Casting

Once you've adjusted your reel, you are ready to cast. But what sort of cast should you use? That depends on where you are and the type of tackle you are using.

Underarm cast

This type of cast is easy to learn and, with a bit of practice, can be extremely accurate. It's the perfect cast for float fishing on canals and rivers and is also very useful when overhanging branches make an overhead cast impossible.

Difficulty ••
Accuracy •••••
Distance •

1 Hold the terminal tackle by the last shot (see page 44) on your line.

2 When you are ready to cast, let go of the shot, lift the tip of your rod and push the rod forward.

3 As the terminal tackle swings past the rod tip, point your index finger. This will release the line and cast your tackle.

Overhead cast

This cast will enable you to reach fish in the deeper water further away from the bank. Take extra care and double check that there is nothing in your way before you attempt this cast.

Difficulty ●●●
Accuracy ●●●
Distance ●●●●

1 Allow a little line off the reel so that your float, ledger or spinner is hanging about 1 m below the tip of your rod.

2 Hold the rod upright with the reel level with the top of your head.

3 Bring the tip of your rod back so the tackle at the end of your line swings out behind you.

4 Now throw the rod forwards!

5 As the tackle flies past the tip of the rod, point your index finger to release the line.

Beach cast

When you are fishing off the beach, you need a powerful cast to get beyond the breaking waves. You can launch your tackle over 100 m with this type of cast but you'll need a proper beach rod, strong line and a heavy sea sinker.

Difficulty ●●●●
Accuracy ●
Distance ●●●●●

Your left hand should be gripping the end of your rod at the same height as your chin.

1 Stand sideways on to the sea with your rod pointing down behind you and your sinker lying on the ground.

3 Release the line as you straighten up and face the sea. Put all your power behind this cast and you'll be able to hurl your tackle right over the surf!

2 When you are ready to cast, swing your shoulders around towards the sea. At the same time, pull your left hand down to your hip and punch your right hand forward.

Pole fishing

When you go fishing with a pole or a whip, you don't use a reel at all. This makes casting very easy!

Difficulty •
Accuracy •••••
Distance – depends on the length of your pole!

1 Using both hands, feed the pole out across the water. Try to keep the pole level but be careful not to drag the tackle through the water as this will disturb the fish.

2 When the tip of your pole is above the spot you want to fish, gently lower your float into the water.

Top tip

If your pole isn't quite long enough to reach the spot you want to fish, try lifting the tip of the pole up just before you lower the float into the water. This will make your line swing out and land further away from you.

Completing the cast

As soon as your terminal tackle hits the water, you must reset your reel to prevent more line coming off the spool. To do this, simply turn the handle. One turn is enough – don't start reeling in the entire line!

If you don't reset your reel immediately, you won't be able to strike if you get an early bite!

You should hear a click as the mechanism responds and, if you're using a fixed-spool reel, you'll see the bale arm flip back into place. What you do next depends on the type of tackle you're using.

Spinning

If you are using a lure that sinks, give it time to reach the depth you want to fish (see page 67) before you start reeling it in.

Float fishing

Wind in any slack line. If you are using a waggler float, don't forget you must submerge the line (see page 42).

Ledgering

Wait until the ledger has sunk to the bottom, then set the rod in its rests and wind in any slack.

Practice makes perfect

The more you practise casting, the better you'll get. But you don't need a lake or a stream to improve your skills. Any wide open space will do. A playground or park is ideal – just make sure that nobody else is within range!

You will need a bucket and a small weight called a plummet. Tie the plummet to your line without a hook, then see if you can cast the plummet into the bucket. Once you start to get the hang of a cast, try varying the distance between you and your target. Then try putting a larger or smaller plummet on the line.

This is an ideal way to spend the closed season (see page 10). Remember, most of the time it's accuracy, not power, that counts in casting. If you can improve your aim, you'll improve your catch!

What to do when it all goes wrong

You're bound to make a few mistakes. When a cast goes wrong, your tackle can end up snared in the branches of a bush or trapped in a thick patch of water weeds. It's going to happen some time, so here's what to do when it does!

Let some line off the reel, then put the rod down on the ground. Wind the slack line around a stick a few times – by pulling the stick, you will be able to pull the line without it cutting into your hands.

As you tug on the stick, keep it away from your face at all times – if you manage to pull your tackle free, you don't want it to fly out and hit you on the head! Gently increase the pressure until your line either snaps or comes away.

What not to do

Don't try to pull the line free using your rod. If you do, as well as losing the tackle at the end of your line, you could also break your rod.

4 Bits and bobs

As well as the absolute essentials (rod, reel, line and hooks), there are lots of other things you can buy to make fishing easier – and more fun. They don't cost a fortune and many are well worth having. Don't buy everything at once. See how your interest in fishing develops. For example, there's no point in buying a rod rest if you just want to go spinning, but a rod rest is useful for float fishing and means that you can start ledgering too.

Spare spools

It is very useful to have a couple of spare spools for your reel, filled with different lines, because you can then change the line you are using in a matter of seconds.

Disgorger

A disgorger will save you a lot of time (and the fish a lot of stress!) when removing awkward hooks. Slip the disgorger on to the line and slide it along until it reaches the hook. When you push the disgorger, you will push the hook back through the hole it has made. When the hook is free, twist the disgorger to turn the hook on its side and carefully pull it out of the fish's mouth.

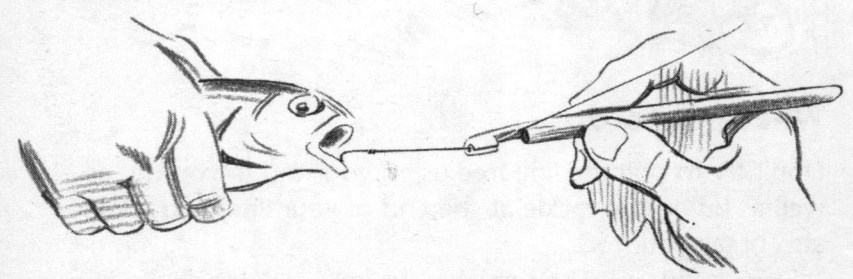

Rod bag

A bag to carry your rod in is well worth having but if you want to spend your money on other things, you can make a rod bag out of an old pair of trousers. Cut the legs off the trousers and sew them together end to end to make a long tube. Fold one end over and sew it up, then sew two rows of stitches along the length of the case – this will stop the three sections of your rod bashing against each other. Fold the top of the case over and keep it shut with some Velcro or a button.

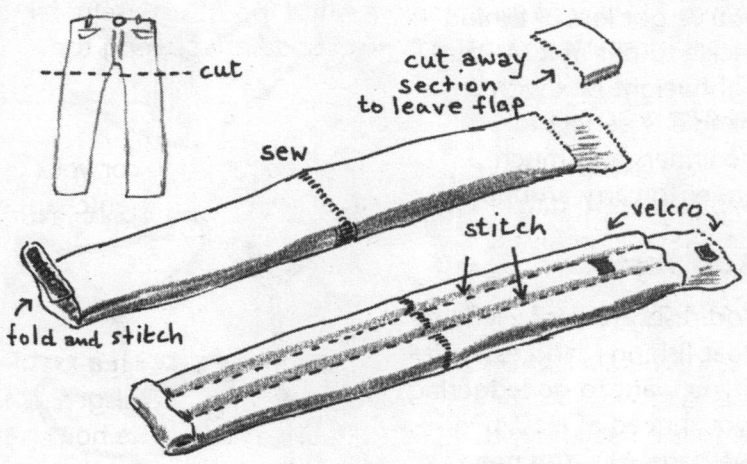

It's a fact!

Sharks are the only fish with eyelids.

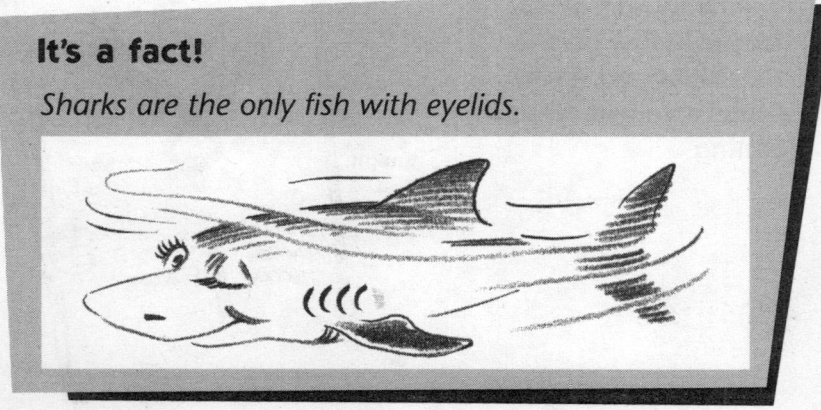

Tackle box

You will need something to keep all your fishing equipment in. Some tackle boxes are big enough to use as seats which makes sitting on the river bank more comfortable, but there's no point in buying a big expensive box until you've got lots of fishing tackle to put in it. A small lightweight box with a handle is perfect for beginners and much easier to carry around.

Rod rests

Rod rests are very useful for float fishing – and essential if you want to go ledgering (you'll need at least two – see page 61). You need a different sort of rest for fishing with a pole. A sea fishing rod rest is useful if you are beach-casting.

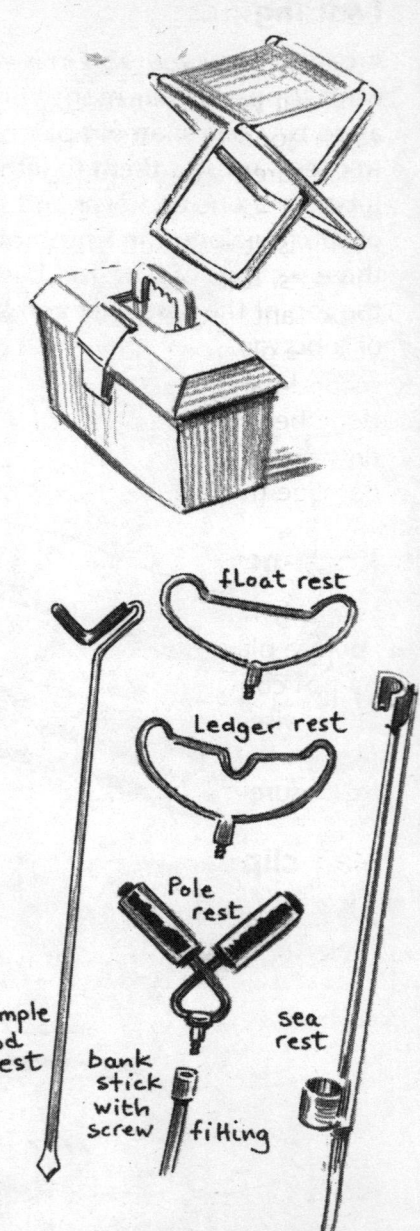

float rest

Ledger rest

Pole rest

simple rod rest

bank stick with screw

fitting

sea rest

Landing net

This is a 'must' for coarse
fishing if you are hoping to
catch good-sized fish. But
make sure that your net is
knotless – in other words,
that it isn't made up of lots
of knots. It is particularly
important to check this if
you are given an old
second-hand net. Old-
fashioned knotted nets are
now illegal as they can
damage the fish's body.

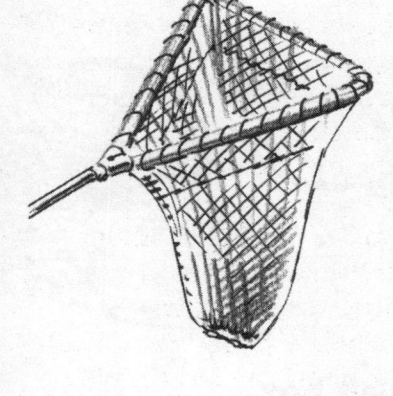

Keep-net

You only need a keep-net if
you are planning on taking
part in competitions.
Otherwise, it's a waste of
money. If you do buy one,
make sure it is knotless.

Nail clippers

Better than a knife for
trimming line.

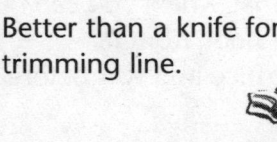

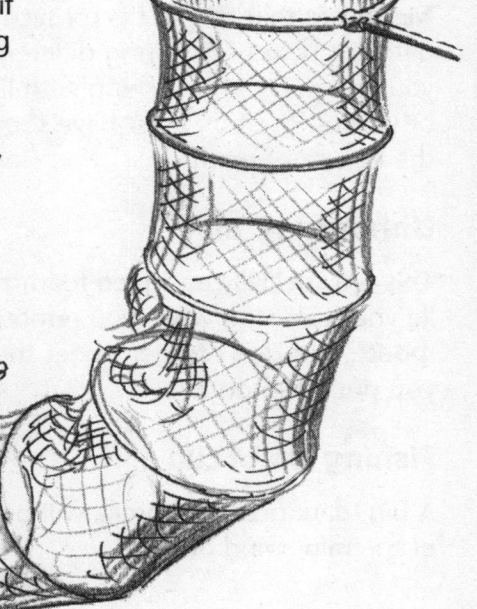

Bait catapult

This is used for groundbaiting (see page 91). It's not essential but it does come in handy.

Bait box

You must have at least one container to keep your bait in. Make sure that the lid fits on securely. Having a couple of different boxes for storing different baits is a good idea. If you are going to be fishing with live bait such as maggots or worms, the box must have some small holes in it so that the bait can breathe.

Unhooking mat

This is a specially designed foam-filled mat which you can lie your catch on while you remove the hook from its mouth. But don't forget to get the mat nice and wet before you put a fish on it.

Fishing umbrella

A big, dark green umbrella will protect you from the worst of the rain, wind or sun.

Float away

Float fishing is the most popular method of coarse fishing. Floats can be used to catch almost any type of fish. If you've never gone fishing before, this is the way to start!

Float fishing in a nutshell

What does a float do? It does two things. It holds your bait at the correct depth in the water where (hopefully!) the fish will find it. It also moves when a fish takes the bait, showing you that you've got a bite.

On the line

Most float fishing is done on a light line – about 2 lb is usually enough for the fish you are most likely to catch, such as roach, rudd or dace.

There are two basic types of float. One is for fishing on still water – water that is moving very slowly or not at all, such as in lakes or canals. The other is for use on rivers where the water flows more rapidly.

It's a fact!

There are 30,000 different types of fish but only 2300 species live in fresh water. The rest live in the sea.

There are plenty more fish in the sea!

Still-water floats

Still-water floats (or wagglers, as they are known) are attached to the line by the bottom only. The line is threaded through an eye on the end of the float and secured in position by two weights on either side.

Most modern floats are plastic but the very best wagglers are made from the quills of peacock feathers or from the stems of a reed called sarkanas.

Insert waggler

This is an extremely sensitive float that will allow you to detect even the smallest nibble from a fish. However, it can only be used on calm water when there is very little wind.

Straight waggler

This is the standard float for fishing on lakes and canals. It can cope with a gentle flow and a breeze.

Bodied waggler

This float uses more shot than other wagglers. The extra weight means that it can be cast much further but it is a less sensitive bite indicator.

Use at least half the total shot on the line as locking shot.

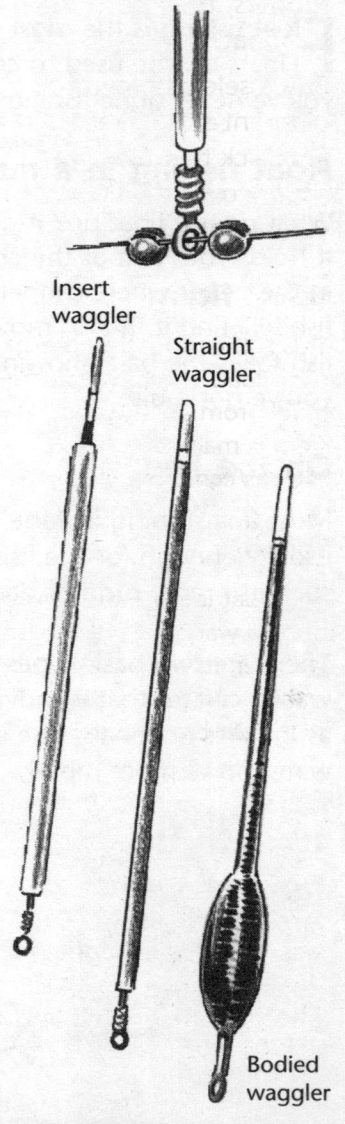

Insert waggler

Straight waggler

Bodied waggler

Floats for river fishing

This type of float is attached to the line by two elastic rings called float rubbers. You thread the line through the rubbers, then push them over the top and bottom end of the float.

Buy a selection of different-sized rubbers and pick two that fit snugly over the float you are using.

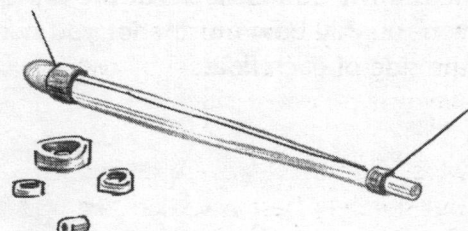

Stick float

This is the most common type of river float. The top of the float is made from balsa wood, while the stem is made of a heavier material such as cane, plastic or wire.

Avon

This float looks like an upside-down bodied waggler. Like the bodied waggler, its extra weight means it can be cast further than a normal stick float but it is also less sensitive.

Balsa

Balsa floats are only used on deep, fast-flowing waters.

River floats have bright tips. These allow you to see the float clearly when you are trotting (see page 51) at a distance.

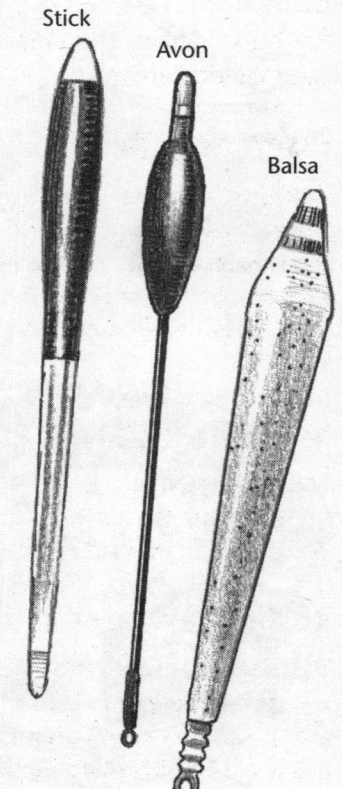

Stick

Avon

Balsa

Get yourself shot!

Only the tip of the float should stick out above the water. This means you need some shot. Shot are small, round weights with a split in them which are used to weigh the float down so that it sits at the right depth. A guide telling you roughly how much shot you need to use is printed on the side of each float.

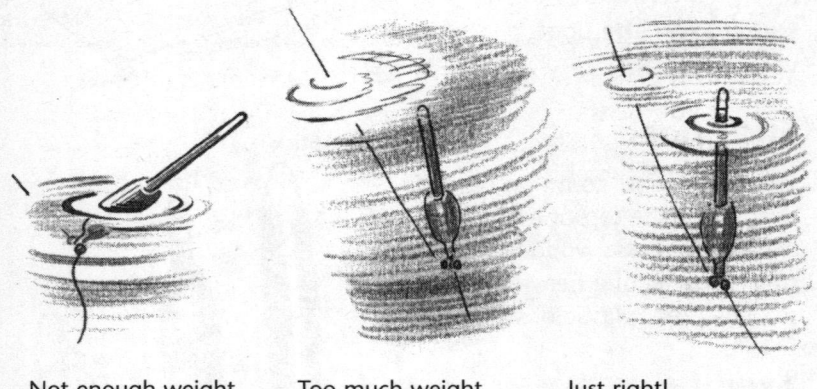

Not enough weight   Too much weight   Just right!

A box with a swivel opening makes it easier to get the weight you want without spilling all the others.

Shot comes in different sizes. Buy a box with a good selection.

Lead alert

Most fishing weights used to be made of lead. However, lead weights can poison birds and fish. It is now illegal to use lead weights that weigh less than 28 g.

If someone has given you their old fishing tackle, make sure the weights are not made of lead. If they are, buy yourself some new ones and do your bit to protect the water wildlife.

You can use shot of different sizes to make up the total weight you need. For example, on a 2BB float (one that needs the same weight as two BB shot), you could use one BB, one No 4, and two No 6. This means that you can spread the shot out between the float and the hook.

The table below will help you work out how the different weights add up.

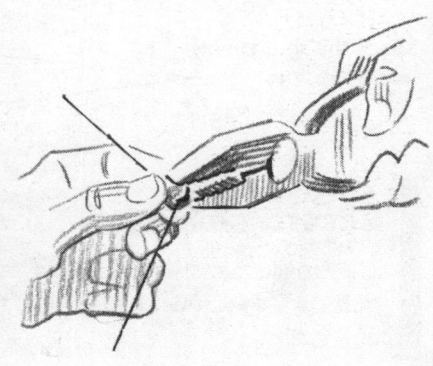

1 SSG = 2 AAA = 4 BB
1 BB = 2 No 4 = 4 No 6
1 No 1 = 2 No 5 = 3 No 6
1 No 4 = 2 No 6 = 4 No 8
1 No 5 = 1 No 6 + 1 No 8
1 No 6 = 2 No 8

Fixing shot to your line

Put your line through the split in the shot. Then gently pinch the shot with a pair of pliers. This will close the split around the line, fixing the shot in place.

Shotting patterns

There are several ways you can arrange the shot on your line. Have a look at some different patterns.

This pattern allows the bait to sink slowly through the water, attracting fish at different depths. It is known as 'fishing on the drop' and requires a sensitive float – an insert waggler is ideal.

Use almost all the weight as locking shot to keep the float in place.

A little weight is placed halfway between the float and the hook.

The last shot on the line is very small. This is called 'dust' shot.

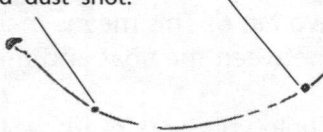

This pattern is used for 'trotting' with a stick float (see page 51). It creates a tail that swings through the water as the float is pulled along by the flow.

Put the largest shot under the float. This makes it more stable.

Space the shot evenly along the line.

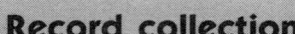

Record collection

The smallest freshwater fish in the world is the dwarf pygmy goby. A fully-grown male is less than 1 cm long. Not much of a catch!

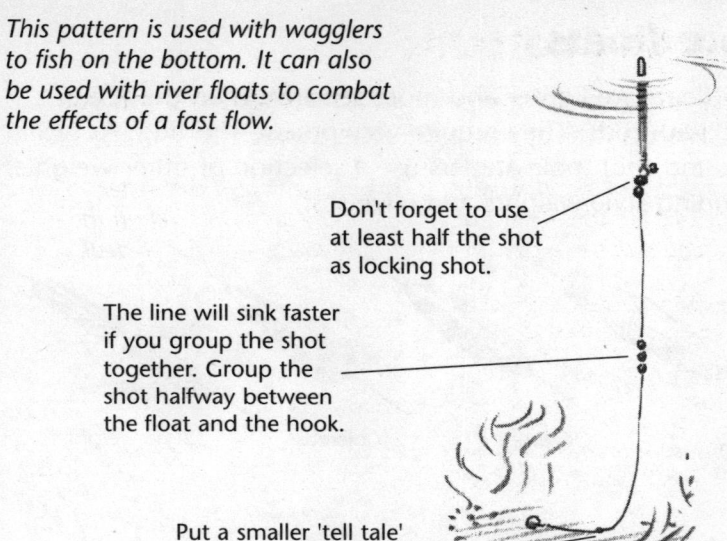

This pattern is used with wagglers to fish on the bottom. It can also be used with river floats to combat the effects of a fast flow.

Don't forget to use at least half the shot as locking shot.

The line will sink faster if you group the shot together. Group the shot halfway between the float and the hook.

Put a smaller 'tell tale' weight near the hook.

The lift method

The lift method is used on still water for fishing on the bottom with larger baits such as bread or sweetcorn. This is the technique to use if you want to catch tench. It's also worth trying for bream. When the bait is taken, the float will rise up and then fall flat on the water.

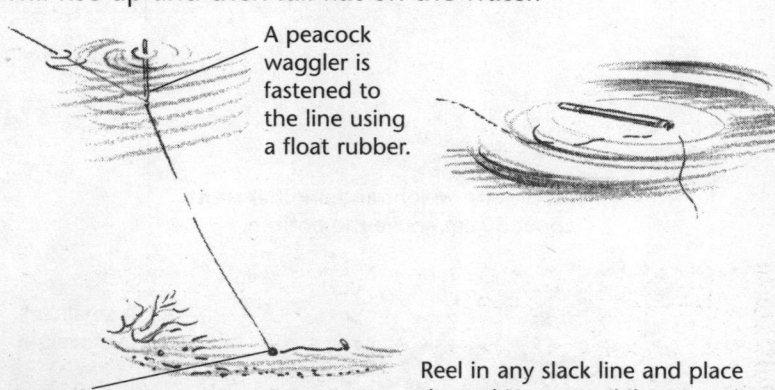

A peacock waggler is fastened to the line using a float rubber.

Fix a single, large shot (SSG or AAA) near the hook.

Reel in any slack line and place the rod in a rest while you wait for a bite.

Pole floats

Pole floats are lighter and more sensitive than the floats used with rods. They require very precise shotting. As well as round shot, pole anglers use a selection of other weights, including style weights and olivettes.

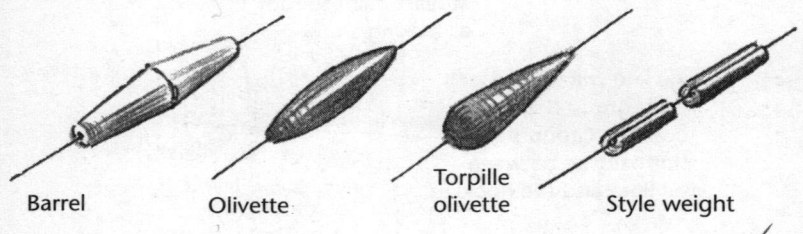

Barrel   Olivette   Torpille
                                  olivette   Style weight

One of the most widely used pole rigs is a balsa bristle rig. This is perfect for fishing in still waters.

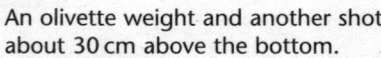

An olivette weight and another shot about 30 cm above the bottom.

A small 'tell tale' weight (a No 8) rests on the bottom.

30 cm between the last shot and the hook.

Finding the bottom

Fish are often to be found near the bottom, especially during the colder months. To make sure your bait reaches them, you must work out the depth of the water, and for this you need a plummet.

Guess the depth and fix a float in position. Attach a plummet to the end of the line and cast into the area you want to fish. If the float lies down, your line is too long. If the float sinks, your line isn't long enough. But if the float sits properly in the water, you've got the depth just right.

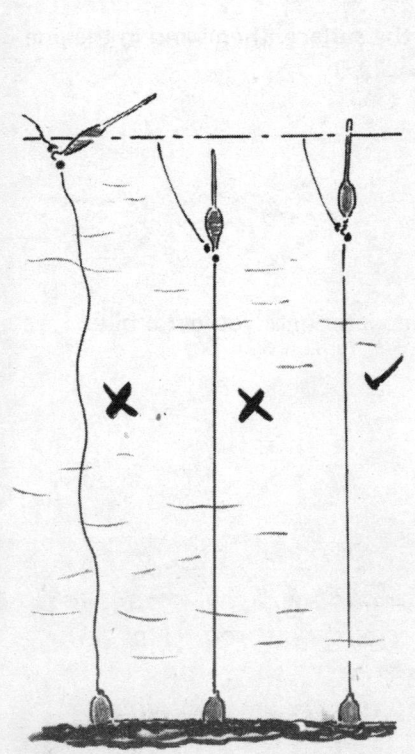

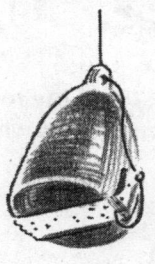

On a traditional plummet, you thread your hook through the eye at the top of the weight then push it into a strip of soft material on the base.

You can also buy clip-on plummets. These are easier to use, but they can fly off the line if you cast too hard!

49

Sinking your line

When you go fishing with a waggler, you must sink your line below the water after each cast. If you don't, your line will lift the bottom of the float and the float won't sit straight. This is how you do it.

1   Cast beyond the area you actually want to fish.

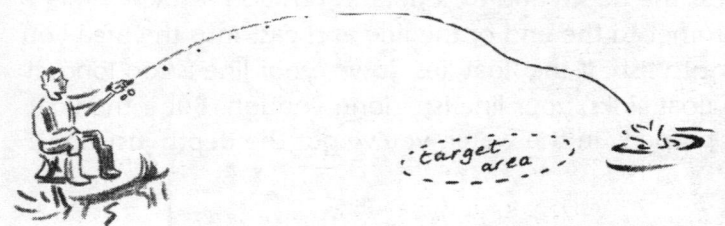

2   Dip the tip of the rod below the surface, then wind in the line until your float is where you want it.

3   Keep the tip of your rod underwater until you get a bite.

Tackle tip

If float fishing is the kind of angling you really want to do, you might want to buy a specialist float rod. Float rods tend to be longer than other coarse fishing rods. A 12-ft rod is ideal unless you are very tall, in which case try a 13-ft rod.

Trotting

Trotting is a technique for fishing on rivers. The idea is to let the float be dragged along by the flow of the water. This is how you do it.

1 When you cast, don't reset your reel. Instead, trap the line against the spool using your finger.

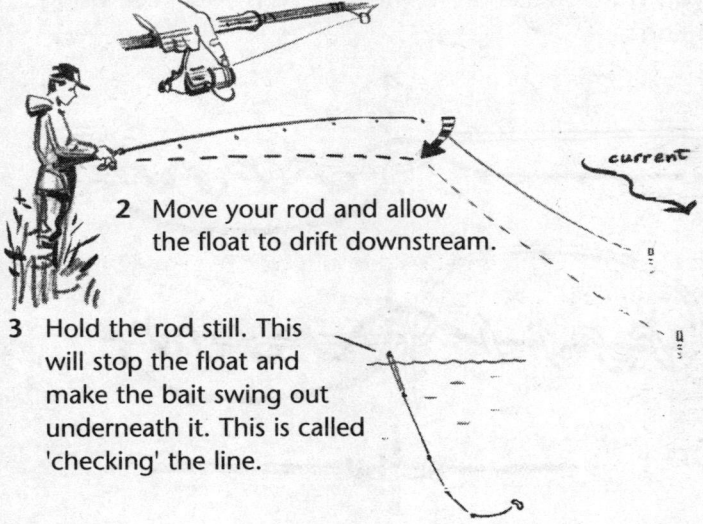

current

2 Move your rod and allow the float to drift downstream.

3 Hold the rod still. This will stop the float and make the bait swing out underneath it. This is called 'checking' the line.

4 Now lift your finger and pull the rod back quickly. As you do this, a few coils of line will slip off the spool.

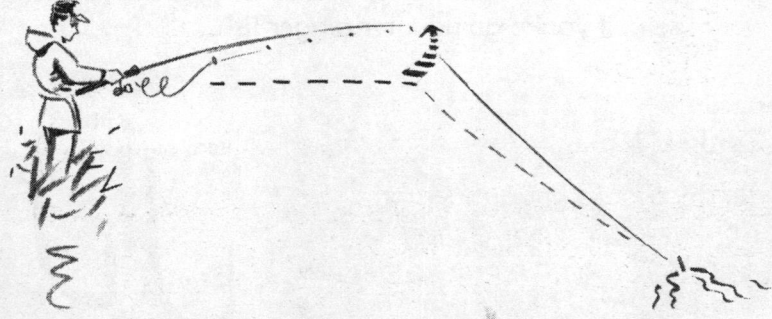

5 Put your finger back in position and let the float start to drift again.

Before you go

It's a good idea to put a selection of your favourite floats on separate lengths of line, complete with hooks and shot. Make sure that each float is weighted correctly by testing it in a bucket of water. This saves a lot of fiddling around on the river bank. All you have to do is tie the line with the float you want to use on to the line from your reel, using a blood knot.

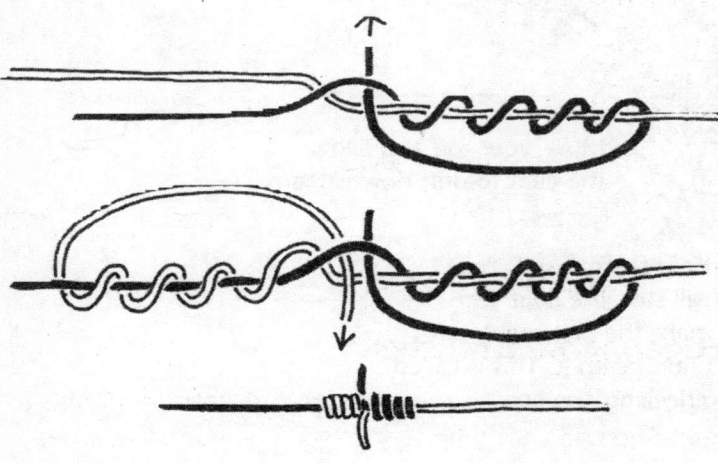

As well as saving time, this allows you to use a light line on your terminal tackle but a heavier line on your reel, which is very useful if you're going after bigger fish.

Tackle tip

Barbed hooks are banned on some waters. Always check before you start fishing – and keep a few barbless hooks just in case!

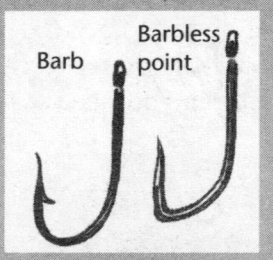

Barb Barbless point

6 Leisurely ledgering

Ledgering is a lazy way to fish – or at least that's what people who have never really tried it will tell you. It may not look like hard work because you spend a lot of time just watching the tip of the rod. But you've got to concentrate, or you'll miss those bites!

Ledgering in a nutshell

A ledger sinks your line down to the bottom and holds it there. The problem with ledgering is working out when you've got a bite. Anglers get round this problem by using extra-sensitive rod tips and special bite indicators.

On the line

Before you go ledgering, make sure your line is strong enough. A light line, suitable for float fishing, is likely to break if you try to cast something as heavy as a bomb ledger. You need a line with a breaking strain of 3-4 lb.

It's a fact!

The largest fish in the world is the whale shark. It can weigh up to 21 tonnes.

Ledgers

Ledgers come in different sizes. For fishing in still water, a ¼ or ½-oz * ledger will do the job but if you're fishing on a river you will need something slightly heavier to stop the current rolling the weight along the bottom. Try a ¾ or 1-oz ledger, depending on the flow.

Remember, a bigger ledger allows you to cast further but also makes a bigger splash and is more likely to scare the fish away.

* Imperial units again! 1 ounce (oz) = 28 g

An Arlesey bomb   A screw bomb

Swan shot

The larger sizes of shot are also used in ledgering, particularly swan shot (also known as SSG).

Swivels

Swivels are used to join lines together. They help to prevent tangles by allowing the lines to turn around freely. Swivels come in different sizes. A No 10 is ideal for ledgering.

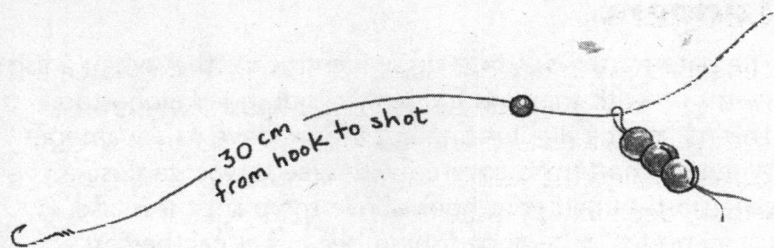

30 cm from hook to shot

Sliding shot rig

A sliding shot rig is a very light rig for use on small rivers and canals. The line with the hook can be pulled by a fish without moving the weight, so the rig is more sensitive and also less likely to scare the fish away.

Use up to four SSG shot attached to a simple loop of line. Put a BB shot about 30 cm from the hook to stop the loop slipping down the line.

Sliding link ledger

This is another sliding rig but it uses a ledger on a length of line. It is a very useful rig for fishing in lakes. The ledger sinks into the silt at the bottom of the lake, leaving the hook free above it.

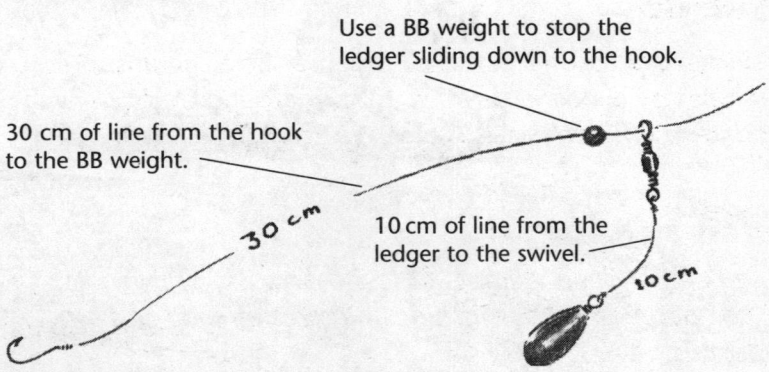

Use a BB weight to stop the ledger sliding down to the hook.

30 cm of line from the hook to the BB weight.

30 cm

10 cm of line from the ledger to the swivel.

10 cm

Paternoster

The paternoster is a fixed rig, which means that when a fish swims off with the bait, the ledger is dragged along too. This makes the rig clumsier but it does have its advantages. When the bottom is covered with weeds, you can use a paternoster to lift your hook above the plants. It is also a useful rig for long-range fishing because it can be cast a good distance.

Adjust the length of line attached to the ledger according to the depth of the weeds. The line with the hook should be about 15 cm long.

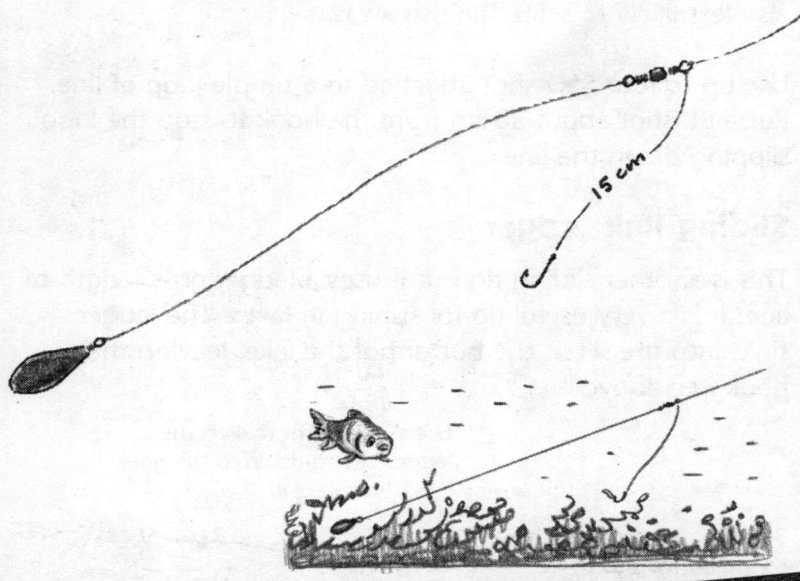

Lead alert

Remember, lead weights of less than 28 g are illegal (see page 45). That includes all sizes of shot and most ledgers.

Swimfeeders

You don't always need a ledger to go ledgering – you can also use a swimfeeder! This is a tube that you fill with bait (usually maggots). In the water, the bait slowly escapes through holes in the tube and attracts fish into your swim.

The weight of the swimfeeder when it's full of bait means that you don't need to use a ledger as well. Set up your tackle as for a sliding link ledger and attach the swimfeeder to the swivel using a clip.

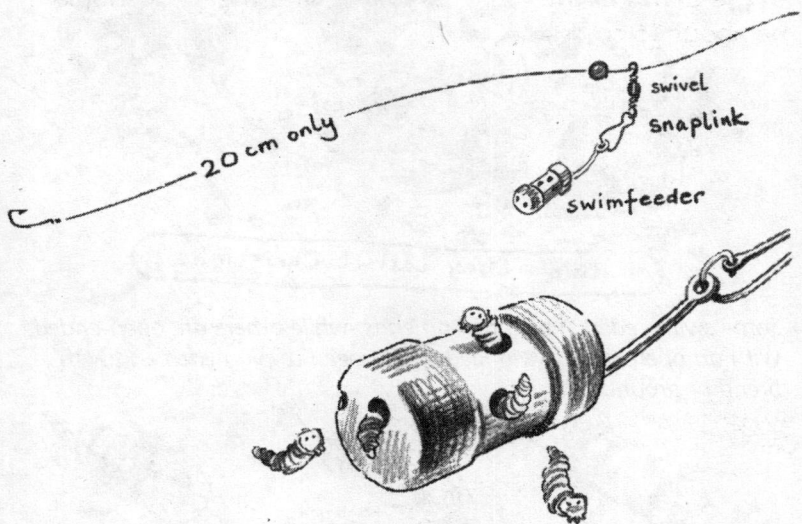

Don't put the hook too far from the swimfeeder – 20 cm of line is enough.

Tackle tip

Once the fish have started to bite, replace the swimfeeder with a ledger. If you don't do this, the fish will simply snap up all the bait from the swimfeeder and ignore what's on your hook!

Casting with a swimfeeder

When you are fishing with a swimfeeder, you must try to hit the same spot with every cast. Remember, the idea is to attract the fish into one area. If the swimfeeder lands in a different place each time you cast, bait will end up all over the place – and so will the fish! This is when time spent practising casting (see page 34) really pays off.

Some swimfeeders have push-on ends, while others are open-ended. With an open-ended swimfeeder, you need to plug each end with bread or groundbait.

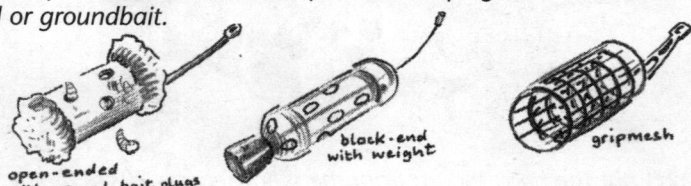

open-ended with ground-bait plugs

block-end with weight

gripmesh

Tackle tip

To slow down the rate at which bait is released by your swimfeeder, put clear sticky tape over some of the holes. Don't forget that too much bait in your swim gives fish a chance to feast without biting your hook.

Watching for bites

When you go ledgering, you haven't got a float to show you when a fish bites the bait. You have to watch the tip of your rod instead. This requires serious concentration – and special rod tips!

The tip of an ordinary rod is too stiff to detect a bite, so what you need is a super-sensitive tip you can screw into the end of your rod. These come in two sorts, swing tips and quiver tips.

KEEP your eyes on the tip of your rod or you might miss something!

A good all-purpose rod has a screw end for attaching either screw or quiver tips (see page 60). But for really keen anglers, there are specialist ledger rods. These are usually about 9–10 ft long (that's shorter than most float fishing rods) and come with built-in quiver tips.

Swing tip

A swing tip dangles down from the end of your rod by a rubber tube. It can swing freely which makes it extremely sensitive. The problem with a swing tip is that it is so sensitive it can only be used on still water in windless conditions.

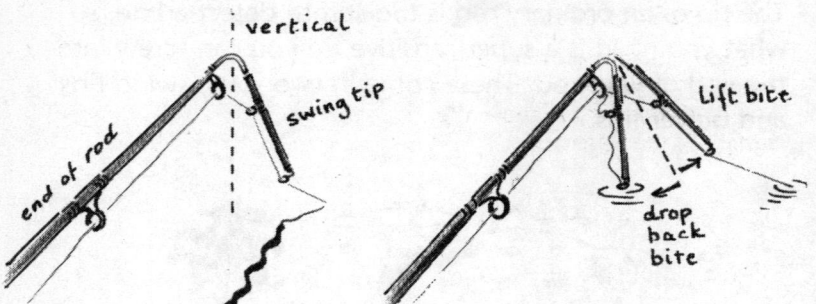

Wind in the line until the tip has been lifted 4 cm.
A swing tip will lift up or drop down when you get a bite.

Quiver tip

A quiver tip sticks out from the end of your rod. It is not as sensitive as a swing tip but has the advantage that it can be used on running water as well as still water.

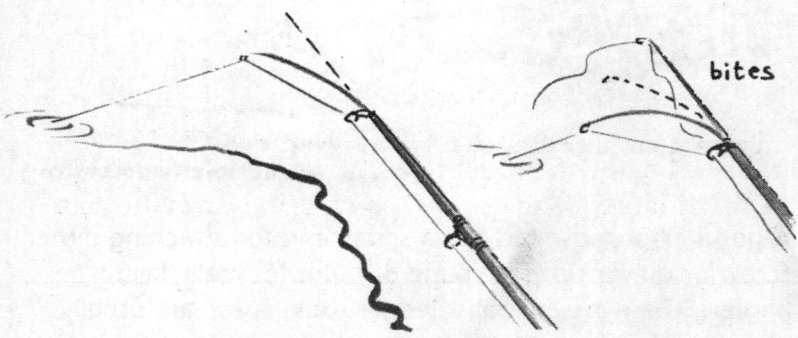

Wind in the line until you get a gentle curve in the tip.
A quiver tip will bend more or straighten up when you've got a bite.

Give your rod a rest!

A swing tip or quiver tip won't work unless your rod is
perfectly still. That's why, if you are going ledgering, you
need at least two rod rests (see page 38). Put your rod into
the rests as soon as you have cast, then wind in the line
until the tip is set correctly. Once you've done this, you
won't need to touch the rod again until you get a bite.

The rod should point downstream,
roughly 45° away from the ledger.
The tip should be just above the
surface of the water.

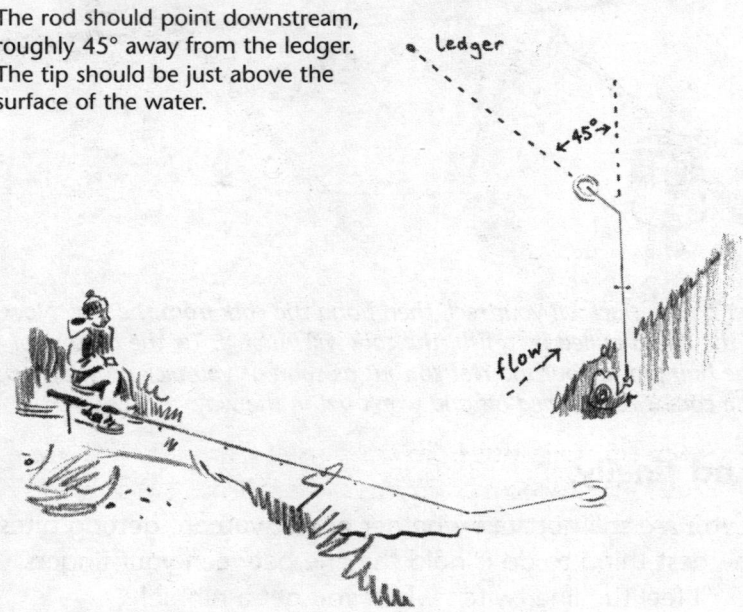

This arrangement is perfect unless you are fishing in a
strong current. If you go ledgering in fast-flowing water,
you must raise your rod up, beachcasting style (see page
79). This lifts the line out of the water and stops the current
bending the tip.

DON'T FORGET
You need to use a quiver tip if you are fishing on water
that's flowing!

Bite indicators

Some anglers also use bite indicators when they are ledgering. These can be useful, especially if you are fishing with more than one rod. You can buy electronic indicators which bleep when you get a bite but you can also make your own indicator using a hair pin pushed through a cork.

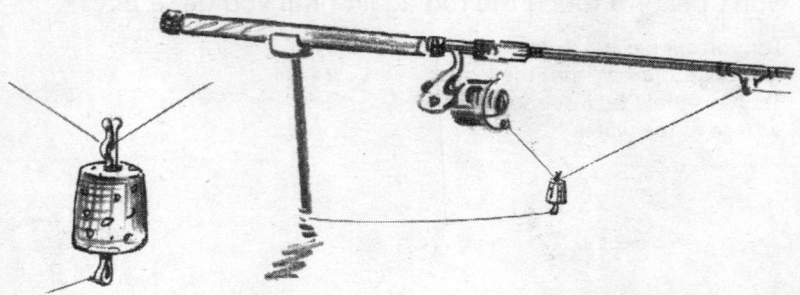

Let a little slack off your reel, then hang the cork from the line. Now, if the line is pulled by a fish, the cork will wobble. Tie the bottom of the hair pin to your rod rest so that as soon as you pick up your rod, the cork will be pulled off and won't get in the way.

And finally...

If you are still not sure whether or not you are getting bites, the best thing to do is hold the line between your fingers. You'll feel the line twitch when you get a nibble!

It's a fact!

Fish eat more when the water is warm. That's because they're more active in warm water.

In a spin

Spinning is a really exciting way to fish because you are busy all the time, constantly casting and retrieving your line. This technique is used to catch pike, perch and zander, which are predators that feed on smaller fish. The best time to go spinning is in winter when other species are less active and success with floats and ledgers becomes harder.

Spinning in a nutshell

Spinning means fishing using an artificial lure that's designed to look like a small fish. Some of these lures spin around as they are pulled through the water, which is how spinning got its name!

On the line

You'll need at least a 5-lb line if you are going spinning for zander, perch or small pike. To catch big pike, you'll need line that's twice as strong – and a specialist rod!

Lures

The three basic types of lure are called spinners, spoons and plugs. Spoons and plugs don't actually spin, although fishing with them is still known as spinning.

Spinners

A spinner has a shiny metal blade that rotates as it moves through the water. When the blade catches the light, it looks like the flickering body of a fish.

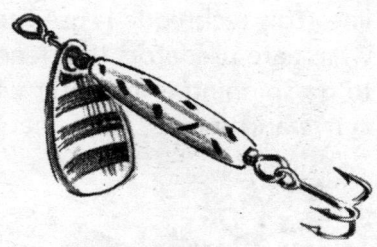

This weight enables the spinner to be cast further.

Spoons

A spoon is a strip of curved metal that wobbles as it is pulled along.

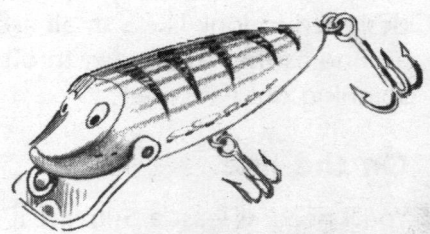

The hooks used on lures have three points and are called treble hooks.

Plugs

Plugs are usually fish-shaped. Most float until you start to retrieve your line. As the plug is pulled along, a vane on the front makes it dive under the surface.

This vane makes the plug dive as you reel in your line.

en,' says Betty, 'said you would tell me where we are as soon as the anchor was up.'

Do you hear that rumble out there? That is the capstan turning and the chain beginning to leave the wet sea for the dry air. That means, yes, I can tell you. We are bound for Tangier, or whatever now remains of it.'

'To see my father? Oh, my prayers are answered . . .'

'Betty, our first task is to find your father.'

Pepys and Hewer have that same thought in mind and are also finally converging on Tangier. Barto has kept his promise as soon as the floods allow and finds them in Seville for their much-delayed return to Sanlucar, more than eight weeks after they left. A carriage takes them on to Cadiz and their first clear view of the harbour is startling because they see half the English warships of Dartmouth's fleet moored there.

It is easy to find the officers in the taverns around the port area, busy about their private business, making lucrative arrangements for those 'good voyages' that Pepys has always abhorred. He cannot see Wyborne or any of the few more honest captains he respects. They are still in Tangier and it is the rogue captains who have slipped away to get here early who are feathering their nests. In his cups, Aylmer boasts to them that he stands to make five thousand pounds from this one very 'good voyage' home. They laugh when Pepys shows them Dartmouth's order commanding any navy ship he encounters to transport him straight back to Tangier. They say they are done with Dartmouth's orders and tell Pepys to shut his mouth and enjoy himself. The *Grafton* and the others will be here soon enough and anyway, what's the point of going back to see a horrible sight?

Pepys and Hewer fume helplessly until, eleven weeks
they left Tangier, news spreads that the *Grafton* and the rest or
the fleet have dropped their anchors in the Bay of Bulls, close
by. It is Pepys's fifty-first birthday but this is not destined to be
a day of any celebration.

Captain Booth meets them when they step on to the *Grafton*'s
deck and makes a face when Pepys asks if Kirke is on board.

'Oh no, sir. We put him and his men into the *Sapphire*. She
has a lively ride though sadly she is unlikely to sink. Did you
want to speak with him?'

'No, I want to strangle him.'

'You are far from alone, but try not to strangle Lord
Dartmouth. He is most keen to see you.'

Dartmouth is beyond exasperation and there is no softer
George Legge to be seen. His lordship is on the very edge of
anger, furious with those corrupted captains who have made
every unlikely excuse to avoid his orders, worn down by the
strain of igniting mines in incessant downpours and desperate
to water the fleet, replenish supplies and get back to England
as fast as possible. He has praise only for the very few people
he still trusts.

'Henry Sheres has done a splendid job. I am sorry you will
not see it. Wyborne has also done much. He would rather stay
poor than make his fortune with these venal captains and he
has brought me some remarkably good news. Now first, did
you find your brother?'

'No. Kirke's thugs have been chasing him. I hoped he might
have found you.'

'Kirke's thugs? Kirke is thankfully gone from here. We
shipped him and his household home early on the *Sapphire*. I

could not stand the man for a moment longer. By his thugs, I take it you mean that band called his lambs?'

'I do.'

'I decided they were best separated from their master. Wyborne bravely volunteered to take them under tight control in the *Happy Return*. He will brook no bad behaviour.'

'So you have not heard from Balthasar?'

'I fear not and that I regret, because I wanted to thank him greatly for his unexpected service. That is what I meant by remarkable news.'

'What service?'

'You did not know? Captain Wyborne uncovered it when these storms split three of his spars and he was forced into the bay of Al Jazera. Do you know what he found? A storehouse of which we knew absolutely nothing, built and equipped by your remarkable brother and staffed by our own English sailors.'

'Jebel Tariq? Under a rock like a massive axe head?'

'That must be it. These sailors are rough men with no care for foreign names. Wyborne says they called it Jebraltar and he agrees with your brother that it will make a safer haven than Tangier ever could.'

'But are you telling me Wyborne did not find my brother there?'

'No he did not. He said the men there were hungry and anxious for news.' He stops and frowns. 'However ... do pardon me. I forgot. A Smyrna merchant came twice in the past week. He had news but was commanded to tell it only to you, to Hewer or to Captain Wyborne. He had those names written down and was fiercely resistant to any suggestion of talking to me or to Captain Booth. I think he had been given rapid instructions in some sort of crisis moment.'

'He gave you no hint at all?'

'All I can say, Samuel, and it pains me, is that he had a sorrowful expression.'

There, at anchor close to Cadiz, Pepys now finds himself utterly stuck. He begs Booth for the loan of a longboat and a few men to take him back to Tangier to find this merchant.

'Impossible,' says Booth. 'The place is entirely in the hands of the Alcaïd's army now. Without a strong force of warships to support you, you would last two minutes at most and Dartmouth will not permit the fleet to split up again. We will be sailing for home very soon. I understand your distress, but . . . with God's grace your brother may find his own way.'

As the fleet prepares, Pepys stays in his cabin or stalks up and down the deck of the *Grafton*, talking to no one, not even Will Hewer. The steward brings him food but he has little appetite as he imagines the wreckage of Tangier and perhaps Balty lying forever somewhere underneath it. He longs to speak to this Smyrna merchant, but Tangier is more than sixty miles away, a dozen hours in any wind less than a hurricane.

Sometimes you get what you wished for and then wish you hadn't. The fleet, thirty-five vessels in total, sails in the early evening of the 26th day of February and the malign gods of the weather have been biding their time. A hurricane comes.

Further north, everyone on the deck of the *Moonstone* can see what lies ahead. They are sailing down the coast of Portugal and by the evening of the first day the sky far off the starboard bow, low on the horizon, is boiling yellow and black. Until then it has been a pleasant journey, heading directly south at six knots by the log, reaching on a steady westerly. At midday, Clifton announces a competition for his officers. A pair of the ship's muskets are brought up to the quarterdeck along with a sack of fishing net floats. These are hollow green glass spheres, half a foot across, each contained in a mesh net. Ezra ties a sounding line to the first one and drops it over the stern, paying out the line so it bobs around, leaping in and out on the wave-tops in their wake. The captain puts up a prize of one gold sovereign to the first to smash two of the floats. One after another they shoot at the jumping target. After Sam and six other men have shot at it and missed, Clifton takes his time, fires, and there are cheers as it flies to piece. Ezra says, 'You can't win your own prize, sir', as he rigs another one, but twenty shots later everyone has missed it and Ezra points at Betty. 'Let her try,' he says and all the other men suppress laughs − all that is except for Sam and Clifton, who simply nod.

Betty hefts the heavy musket as she watches the behaviour of the waves for a minute or two, then lifts it to her shoulder and aims as the ball is surfing across the top of one steady wave, shattering it. 'You wanted two hits?' she says and Ezra passes her the other musket. This time she has to wait a little longer for the right wave, but the result is the same. The float bursts apart, the startled officers applaud and Ezra hands her the heavy coin. 'There you go, gents,' he says, 'she is a good shot and she is more clever than all of you.'

Now the entire crew switches its attention to the threatening sky. By the time full darkness falls they come abreast of the lonely fortress at Sagres on the south-western tip of Portugal, the cape named by the Romans as the most sacred end of the

world. That darkness is illuminated by flashes in the thick
clouds creeping up astern. They bear away to run eastward
along the coast towards the Spanish border and Cadiz and at
midnight, the greatest storm of the entire fierce winter hits.

Dartmouth's fleet is clawing away from land somewhere
ahead of them, struggling under storm sails and scattered at
the whim of the weather gods. In the early hours the *Grafton*
suffers catastrophic damage to its spars and rigging. Ship after
ship struggles up under her stern to report their condition and
receive orders. Three frigates and six smaller merchant ships,
already showing significant damage, are ordered to head for
the shelter of this unexpected depot under the great rock of
Jebraltar in the hope the stores there will have what they need.
Five of the rest, including Wyborne's *Happy Return*, have disappeared somewhere into the storm. The remainder are ordered
to follow the *Grafton* and take the line of least resistance as they
make an unexpected return to the bay of Tangier.

So it is that Samuel Pepys claws his way on deck at dawn on
the last leap year day of February to find the wind has eased from
gale force to merely strong. He is surprised that he does not feel
sick and suspects his body has been too shocked to give its usual
response to rough weather. Will Hewer is already there and they
both stare from the bows towards the city opening up before
them as the *Grafton* limps into the familiar bay. The southern
hills are as they were on that first arrival, climbing to mask the
view of Africa beyond. Memory clings on somewhere behind
their eyes, anticipating the waterfront a mile ahead with the
Devil's Tower to the left and high walls marching right across
to the bulk of Yorke Castle, but memory has been overruled.

They are confronted by an alien scene of utter annihilation as if centuries have passed, not weeks. The fortifications are low heaps of broken stone. Those red-tiled, white walls of the town's crowded houses climbing the slope to the far walls have utterly disappeared. The earthly remains of the market, of forty taverns, four hundred houses, two churches and all else that has served thousands of intruding soldiers all these years have dissolved into formless wreckage, merging grey and brown into the rock below them. For more than two decades the Peterborough Tower has soared upward from the furthest corner, the high point of the city. For all those years it has flown King Charles's flag intended to intimidate the inhabitants of that land, but serving mostly to infuriate. Now the high bastion on which it had stood is utterly empty. The tower and the governor's grand mansion, those symbols of English domination, have been erased, while the sand hills and the rock beyond them assert themselves as they have always done – the natural state of things.

All that remains of the mole is a scatter of humps in the water, shining briefly black between the waves. Those same waves march on, erasing the anchorage as they splash on the broken stone blasted across it to deny shelter to corsair ships. That is all that is left of a third of a mile of massive stonework topped by warehouses and gun batteries, hailed as England's building wonder of the age. They see tiny figures wandering in the ruins, sunlight showing they are Moors by the bright white cloth of their alhaque gowns. Their vast encampment has moved much closer in, held back only by the chaos of the ruins.

'You are thinking of Balty,' says Hewer.

'Of course. I have failed him again. I fear Kirke's lambs found him and did for him.'

Hewer stays quiet, then he points further to the east towards the very far end of the bay. 'Is that not a frigate right down there?'

It is hard to see into the rising sun. 'It must surely be one of our fleet,' says Pepys. 'That is good news.'

Hewer is shading his eyes, but he shakes his head. 'Look, there's a boat coming out.' He points towards the sands around Old Tangier where one of the fishing boats is hoisting a sail. They watch it bounce through the surf then steady its course, directly bow-on. 'I think it's heading for us.'

On two scraps of sail, the *Grafton* slowly passes to the north side of the ruins towards the anchorage off where the Peterborough Tower used to stand. The ship has turned away from the chaos of the mole. The anchor chain clanks out from the capstan and the ship drifts to a halt. They can no longer see past the wreckage of the city to that other frigate, hidden in the bay beyond it.

The fishing boat has followed them round the corner of the city. It comes alongside and an elderly man climbs the ladder at surprising speed. He is intercepted as he steps on deck by a young lieutenant who holds him by the arm and barks questions at him. The man is not wearing an alhaque. He is dressed in the more colourful clothes of the Smyrna traders who pass through from time to time, with a circular red-striped hat on his head and a green and ochre cloak. Pepys crosses the deck towards him and hears the man repeating the word 'Pepps' insistently.

'He means me,' he says to the lieutenant and points at his own chest. 'Yes. I am Pepys.' He turns to Hewer, 'This must be the merchant his lordship spoke of. He came twice after we left.'

The man looks him up and down, uncomprehending, and

thrusts a piece of parchment at him. 'Come with this man' is all it says in rough script.

'Will, could he have Balty's book perhaps?' says Pepys and looks hard at the merchant. 'You have something for me?' he says, gesturing at the man's robes and holding out his hands as if to receive a gift.

The man clutches at them and the lieutenant moves to intervene, but Pepys stops him. He raises his own hands, palms up, and tilts his head to one side in silent interrogation. The man beckons him, points down towards his boat and then ashore, trying to lead him to the ladder. Pepys nods. 'Will,' he says, 'come with me if you please.' He turns to the lieutenant. 'Send someone at once to rouse Captain Booth. Not you. Watch where this man takes us if you can and send some men after us, but I do think he is a friend.'

The wind is now veering all over the compass and the merchant is struggling with the tiller, slowly getting back to the place he came from, the sands by the ruins of Old Tangier, where they see fishermen tending their boats while another walks the shoreline, gathering driftwood to cook the meal that may follow.

The merchant leads them to a half-circle of old Roman building stones and gestures to them to sit while he goes into the trees. Will Hewer is squinting across the bay at the distant ship, becoming clearer now the sun is no longer directly behind it. 'It's one of our frigates, all right, and I think there's a long-boat coming our way.'

The longboat is too far to make out the details, but it seems to be coming directly towards them. 'Damnation,' says Hewer, 'what I would give for a glass.'

'It's not the *Sapphire*, is it?' Pepys says, suddenly nervous. Could Kirke have somehow contrived to return? If it is his men in that longboat with Balty's book of evidence about to be produced from somewhere in the woods, then they are entirely unprotected on this beach with not a weapon between them. Neither of them buckled on their swords this morning. How stupid, he thinks, after all this.

'No,' says Will staring into the distance. 'I think it is the *Happy Return.*'

'Is it? Will, that has Kirke's lambs on board. It's not Monahan and his murderers in the longboat, is it?'

'Samuel, be calm. John Wyborne commands it and he will have them secure. He has a hundred loyal sailors with him.'

For perhaps ten minutes, they stare at the slowly approaching boat, and back the other way, hoping to see the *Grafton*'s boats coming to support them, but instead they are astonished to hear a cannon fire. Another frigate, full sail set, is coming at speed in from the open sea, the smoke from either a salute or a warning shot dissipating fast as it is whirled away. The ship swings up into wind, sails flapping, and drops anchor. They can see men running to lower a boat.

'My god,' says Hewer, aghast. 'That is the damned *Sapphire*. Kirke and his thugs must have control. He's coming for us.' He looks back the other way. 'Come on Wyborne. We need you.'

'Which will get to us first?' says Pepys. 'What can we do?'

'Uh oh,' says Hewer twisting round at a noise behind them. 'Oh no. Who's this?'

The fisherman who was collecting firewood has dropped it in a heap and is running towards them in great leaps across the sand. The low morning sun glints off the blade held in his outstretched hand. Hewer thrusts Pepys behind him, searching the beach with his eyes for anything that might make a weapon. The man with the knife is almost on them, then as Hewer raises a hopeless fist, he runs straight past them and stands, panting, between them and the boats heading towards the shore. 'Run for the town,' he shouts. 'Hide in the ruins. I will slow them,' and Pepys knows that voice very well indeed.

'Balty? My brother? You live?'

'Yes, but not for long unless we all run.' He shoots a quick glance at Pepys. 'Oh no. You won't make it, will you?' He glares at the nearer ship and the boat it has just launched and then away at the distant one whose boat has now reached the shore further along the sand, four men jumping on to the sands and running towards them. They are brandishing long weapons, but whether those are muskets or blades is impossible to tell at this distance.

'Balty, this is the *Sapphire*,' says Pepys, pointing at the nearer ship whose longboat is halfway to the beach, pulling hard. 'It has Kirke and his men on board. That one in the distance is the *Happy Return*. Wyborne is sending us help.'

'Are you sure?' Balty stares at the further ship. 'You're right about that one, it's the *Happy Return* right enough, but ...' he looks back to inspect the new arrival. 'You're wrong about this one,' he says. '*Sapphire* has a shorter mainmast. Brother, this one is Clifton's *Moonstone* and to my mind the men from Wyborne's ship don't look in the least bit helpful.'

'Why do you say ... my god almighty!'

Two of the men from the *Happy Return* have dropped to their knees perhaps five hundred feet away and raise what are now clearly muskets, while the others keep running. They see both muzzles flash. The bang and the balls arrive at almost the same time, one throwing up a spray of sand next to Balty and the other raising a yelp from Will Hewer, who clasps his thigh. The remaining two men, a hundred feet nearer now, drop to their knees to take aim while the first pair reload.

The *Moonstone*'s boat has run its nose up the beach. Six rowers release their oars while two other sailors jump over the bows into the shallows and quickly wade to the sand, each holding a pair of long guns up away from the water. The first of them drops to his knees, takes rapid aim and fires, and they see one of the distant group double over and fall flat. He picks up the other gun and calmly drops the next would-be assassin with an equally deadly shot. The second of the *Moonstone*'s crew doesn't try to fire. He simply passes another gun to the kneeling man and then repeats the trick. Four bodies lie still on the sand.

The two sailors run up the beach towards them and the first to get to them is Sam. 'Papa,' he says, 'are you all right? Uncle Pepys, how are you?'

'Unharmed thanks to your marksman friend,' says Pepys.

'But look at poor Mr Hewer,' says the other sailor, the deadly marksman, and at the sound of that unexpected voice, the men all turn their heads and see the long dark hair hanging down from under the cap. 'Don't look like that,' says Betty. 'Who did you think it was?'

CHAPTER 34

The Alcaïd's forces are watching from all around the remains of the city walls and starting to move along the sand towards them, so they think it time to get back in the *Moonstone*'s longboat, helping support a limping Will Hewer. By the time they are back to safety, the frigate is weighing anchor and turning slowly to head for the *Grafton* as the surgeon cleans Will Hewer's wound in the stern gallery, Hewer proclaiming loudly that it is merely a scratch. When the surgeon leaves, Clifton comes to each of them in turn, staring silently into their eyes and pressing their hands between his, until he reaches Betty and Sam. He turns to face them and bows down, then he looks at all five of them and exhales deeply.

'This may be unpalatable for some to hear,' he says, 'but unless those men somehow managed to render John Wyborne and his entire crew immobile, we have to change our minds about the trustworthiness of honest Captain Wyborne. I will speak to Lord Dartmouth by myself on that subject as I doubt he will wish to address it publicly.'

Pepys nods. 'I have never believed it before today, but there are those who have said that Wyborne played a strange part in the *Gloucester* wreck, even perhaps helped to contrive it. That seemed to me absurd, but now I think the scales have fallen from my eyes. That is most shocking. He certainly took the lead in trying to blame good Captain Gunman for the whole affair afterwards. At the time, I attributed that to some effect of the catastrophe on his mind – but now?' He looks at Clifton. 'Dartmouth talks of a "secret of the captains". Remind him of it. This perhaps might be what he means.'

'I will. Now, sir, we must take you and good Mr Hewer to the *Grafton* where you will have a greater degree of comfort than I can provide here.'

'Balty,' says Pepys, 'where is your ledger of Kirke's crimes? He may still contrive to kill you if he thinks he can destroy it.'

Balty turns to look at Will Hewer. 'The house you stayed in caught fire, did it not?'

'Indeed it did.'

'But you saved all your books and documents?'

'Yes.'

'Where are they now?'

'Safe in the hold of the *Grafton*.'

'Look for one with an inscription on the outside covers that says "Seventy Six Mathematical Exercises to Improve the Mind". I was quite sure that if they found it they would not open it.'

When the laughter stops, Clifton turns to look at Betty. 'I must return this remarkable person to her queen at Lisbon in the hope that she has a few less testing days there. However, Betty, I remind you that you are wearing two badges and must complete the tasks given to you by your king and your queen.'

He pulls out a drawer and hands her the two documents.

'They are both for you, Uncle Pepys,' she says, 'but you receive this first one from me as king's messenger on behalf of King Charles. Will you read it now please?'

Pepys carefully breaks the seals, reads the document and then goes back to the start and reads it all over again. He stares at it, shaking his head, and Betty prompts him. 'Tell us please.'

'The king has ... he has ... he has accepted his queen's view that what he terms my remarkable gifts must be used to serve our country better. I am to be appointed once more to be controller of the navy's affairs as soon as we reach London.' He jumps as they start to clap, then his eyes seem to glisten suddenly as Balty hugs him.

'The other one?' Clifton says to remind Betty.

'Oh yes, now you have to blink your eyes and see me in a different form as queen's messenger on behalf of Queen Catherine.' She gives Pepys the second document and as he breaks the seals, she quickly glances at her father. Balty looks exhausted, gently pleased but also out on the far edges of all this as he has been so many times in his life, helping everything happen as it should and seeing other people get the credit for it.

Pepys reads it through, then closes his eyes for a moment, nods his head and holds it out to Balty. 'Brother,' he says, 'please read this to us.'

Balty frowns as he deciphers the florid writing. 'To our loyal Mr Pepys. I, your queen, am aware that you are to be given a free choice of all those you appoint to the Admiralty Commission to support you in preserving and reforming our navy. I have urged one stipulation and that is that you, as soon at it becomes possible, appoint a man to join your commission who has the deepest experience of all that goes wrong in our yards and on our ships. That man is ...' Balty stops and stares at it.

'Go on,' say Pepys and Betty in unison.

Balty stares at both of them. 'That man is ... your brother, Balthasar St Michel.'

Don't get in a twist

If you are using a lure that spins, you need to attach something to your line to stop it getting twisted. There are different sorts of anti-kink devices. Those with weights help you cast the lure further, but if your tackle is too heavy, your spinner will sink like a stone!

Anti-kink vane

Spiral weight

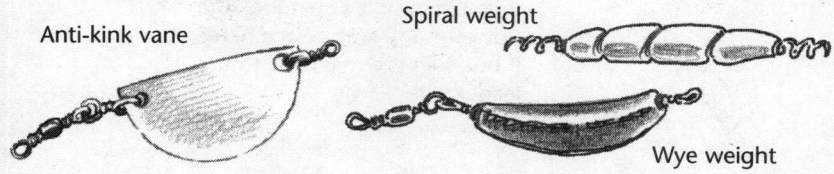

Wye weight

It's a fact!

Some plugs have balls inside them which rattle as they are pulled along. This sound actually attracts the fish. Fish are very sensitive to sounds. They can hear someone on the river bank up to 12 m away – so keep quiet when you're fishing!

Terminal tackle

It's a good idea to use about 20 cm of heavier line between the lure and your reel line. This is called a leader or trace and it is designed to stop the fish biting through the line – don't forget, zander and pike have sharp teeth! Anglers fishing for really large pike usually use a leader made of wire but for smaller predators such as perch, zander and chub an 8-lb mono line will be enough.

The line on your reel should be no less than 5 lb.

reel Line

Leader

If you are using a spinning lure, put your anti-kink device here. If not, join the main line to the leader with a swivel.

A swivel with a clip on the end of your line allows you to change your lure quickly. This is a good idea because you may want to try out several different lures during a day's spinning.

Judging the depth

If you are fishing with a spoon or a spinner, use your first cast to work out the depth of the water. Cast as normal but don't reset your reel. The moment your spinner hits the water, start counting how many seconds it takes to reach the bottom. As the spinner sinks, it will pull line off the spool. Stop counting as soon as the line stops coming off.

Now you know the depth at the bottom, you can fish 'through' the water. Each time you cast, allow the spinner to sink for one more second than on your last cast until you are fishing just above the bottom, then start again near the surface.

There'll be penguins in here next!

It's a fact!

In colder weather, fish tend to move down into the deeper water near the bottom.

Tactics

There's a lot more to spinning than simply winding in your lure after each cast. You must work hard if you want to catch anything. After all, you have to make a lure made of metal, wood or plastic look like an appetising snack to a hungry fish! Here are some tips to help you.

1 Vary the speed of your retrieve. Speed up suddenly with three or four quick turns of the handle, then stop winding altogether and allow the lure to flutter down (or float up, if it's a plug) for a few seconds before continuing.

2 Always keep your rod pointing towards the lure as you draw in the line. If you don't, you may miss a strike.

3 Every now and again, twitch the tip of your rod sideways. This will make the lure dart through the water very realistically. But be careful not to jerk the rod too hard – a light flick with your wrist is all that is needed.

4 When you get a bite, strike slightly harder than you would if you were float fishing or ledgering (see page 95). You need to drive the hooks home as pike, perch and zander are quite good at spitting them out!

path of fast spinning lure

flutter down

darts to side

Yum!

speed up again

Choosing the right lure

Spinners, spoons and plugs come in all sorts of fancy
designs. Some are painted dazzling colours, while others
have reflective plastic discs, bright feathers, beads and even
rotating fins. Just remember that what looks good to you
may not be so attractive to a fish!

A lure that's too big is likely to scare the fish – not catch them!

Size

The most common mistake is to use a lure that's much too
big. The larger lures are only used to catch monster-sized
pike and for this you really need a specialist rod. For
catching more manageable fish, a lure that's 4 cm long is
quite big enough.

Tackle tip

*Don't be fooled by fancy coloured lures. Most fish are
colour blind!*

Colour

Look at the water when you are choosing which lure to use. A shiny silver spinner will work well in dark, murky water in overcast conditions. But if the water is crystal clear and the Sun is shining you need a spinner that is not so bright. Try a gold or red one.

It's like Alton Towers in here

How deep a plug goes when you pull it through the water depends on the angle of the vane on its nose and how fast you reel in your line. The steeper the vane is and the faster you wind, the deeper the plug will dive. Some plugs have adjustable vanes so you can set the depth yourself.

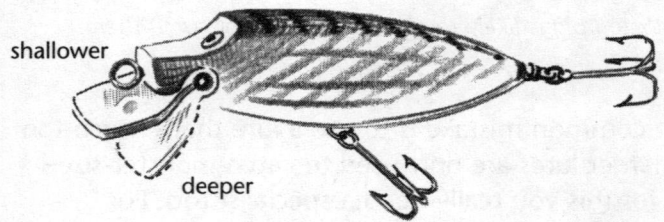

shallower

deeper

Pick and mix

It's a good idea to have a selection of different lures. If you don't get any bites with one, swap it and try another. Be prepared to change your tackle frequently. This is when a clip on your line (see page 66) really saves time.

Rods for spinning

A spinning rod uses a fixed-spool reel.

If you get hooked on spinning, you'll want to buy a rod that's designed for the job. Spinning rods are usually smaller (about 6 ft) and lighter than other fishing rods. This is so that you can cast again and again without getting tired. You can also use a type of rod called a baitcaster, which has a short handle with a trigger grip. The reel on a baitcaster is mounted above the handle and the line runs along the top of the rod. However, if you are interested in landing seriously big predators, you would be better off with a super strong carp or pike rod.

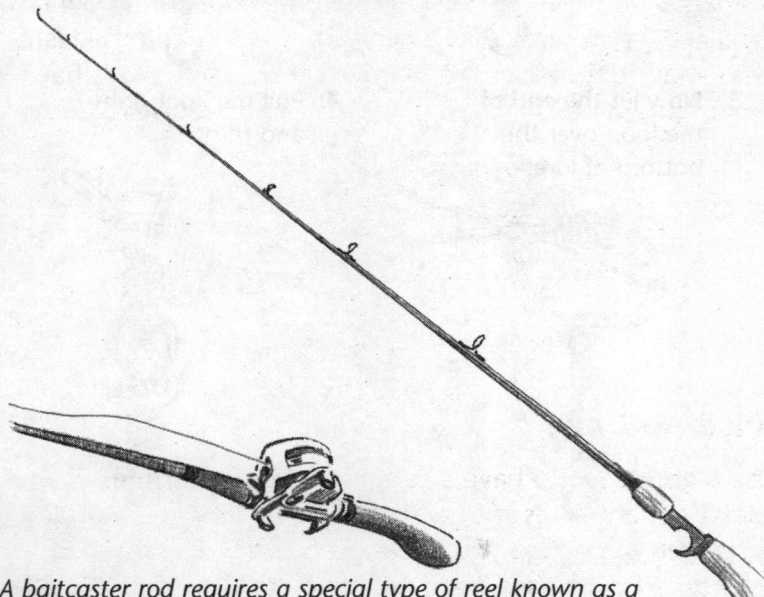

A baitcaster rod requires a special type of reel known as a multiplier (see page 81).

Knot spot

You can use a locked half blood knot (see page 22) to tie your spinning tackle but this technique is worth a try too. It's called the palomar knot and it is just the job for tying a line to a swivel or lure. It's not nearly as hard as it looks!

1 Make a loop of line and pass it through the eye of the lure.

2 Then make a ring and push the end of the loop through it.

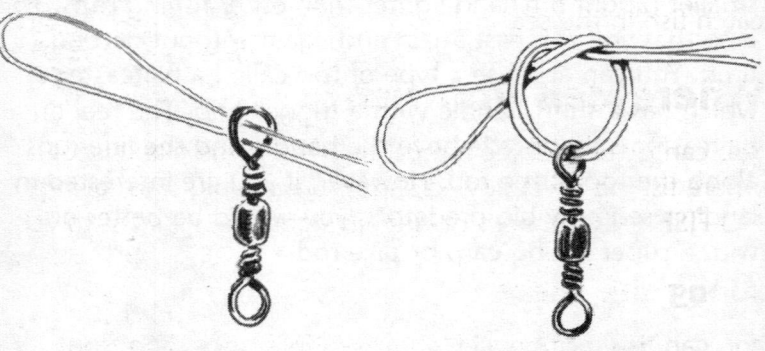

3 Now lift the end of the loop over the bottom of lure.

4 Pull the knot tight and trim.

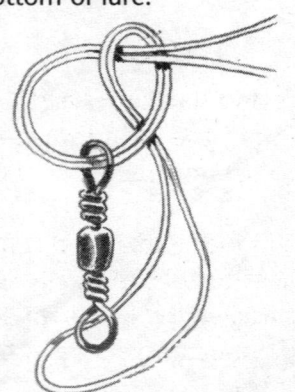

8 Sea dogs

In the last three chapters, you learned how to use floats, ledgers and spinners to go fishing in fresh water. In this chapter, you will learn how to use the same types of tackle to catch fish in the sea.

Where can you fish?

You can go sea fishing almost anywhere you like. Places where fishing isn't allowed should have a big sign saying NO FISHING. If there's no sign in sight, then it's OK to fish.

Along the shore

You can fish for free all along the shore, including from beaches and estuaries (an estuary is a place where a river meets the sea).

Piers and harbour walls

Fishing is banned on a few piers and harbour walls. On some, you have to buy a ticket from the local fishing club but there are lots where you can fish for free.

Just because you can go fishing in lots of places doesn't mean that they are all good places to fish. It's really worth popping into a tackle shop and asking the locals for some expert advice. They will tell you where anglers have had good catches recently.

Safety first

All the normal safety rules (see page 12) apply to sea
fishing – and a few new ones too! The sea can be much
more dangerous than inland waters, so take extra care.

Don't let the rising waters sneak up behind you!

Watch out for tides

It's easy to get trapped by the rising tide. Make sure you're
not fishing in front of a gully that will fill up with water
when the tide comes in. Don't forget that the times of high
and low tides change each day, so it is a good idea to buy
yourself a tide timetable.

Don't go rock climbing

You might see adults climbing across rocky outcrops to go
fishing – but adults are always doing stupid things! These
rocks are sharp and slippery and they can get hit by
unexpected big waves which you won't see coming until
it's too late.

Watch out for swimmers!

Don't fish where people are swimming in the water. You
could cause a serious injury. And keep an eye out for boats,
especially if you are fishing off a sea wall or pier.

Floats for sea fishing

Floats for sea fishing are bigger than most coarse fishing floats, although you could use a pike float (see page 90). The best place to go float fishing is off a pier or sea wall. Don't waste your time float fishing from a beach – even if you manage to cast far enough to reach the fish, you won't be able to see the float!

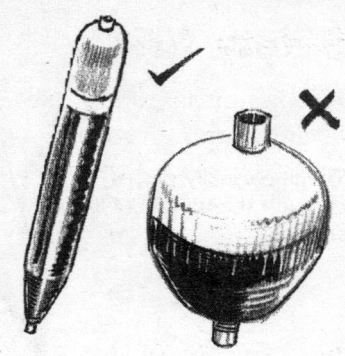

Don't choose a float that is almost round because the fish then has to pull very hard on the line to pull the float under.

Where the fish hang out

You'll find different species of fish at different depths. Change your bait (see chapter 9) and the length of your line to suit what you're hoping to catch.

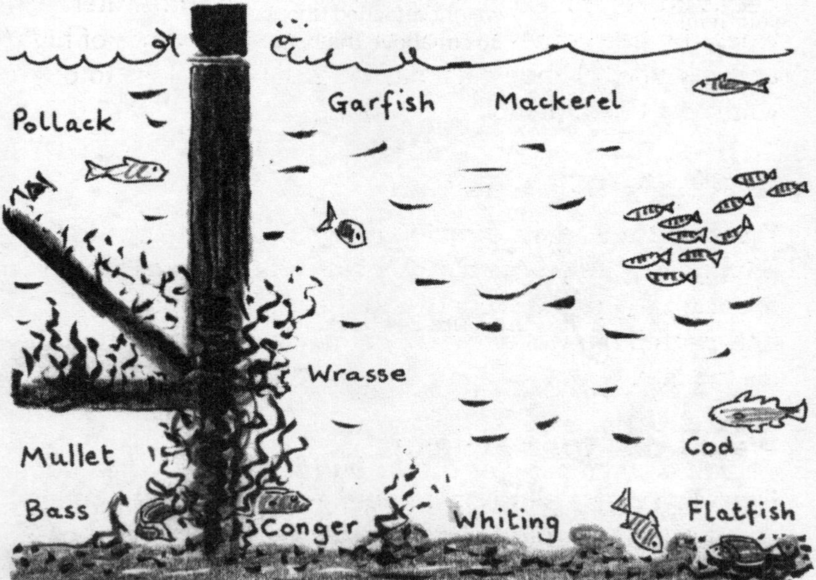

Pollack

Garfish   Mackerel

Wrasse

Mullet   Cod

Bass

Conger   Whiting   Flatfish

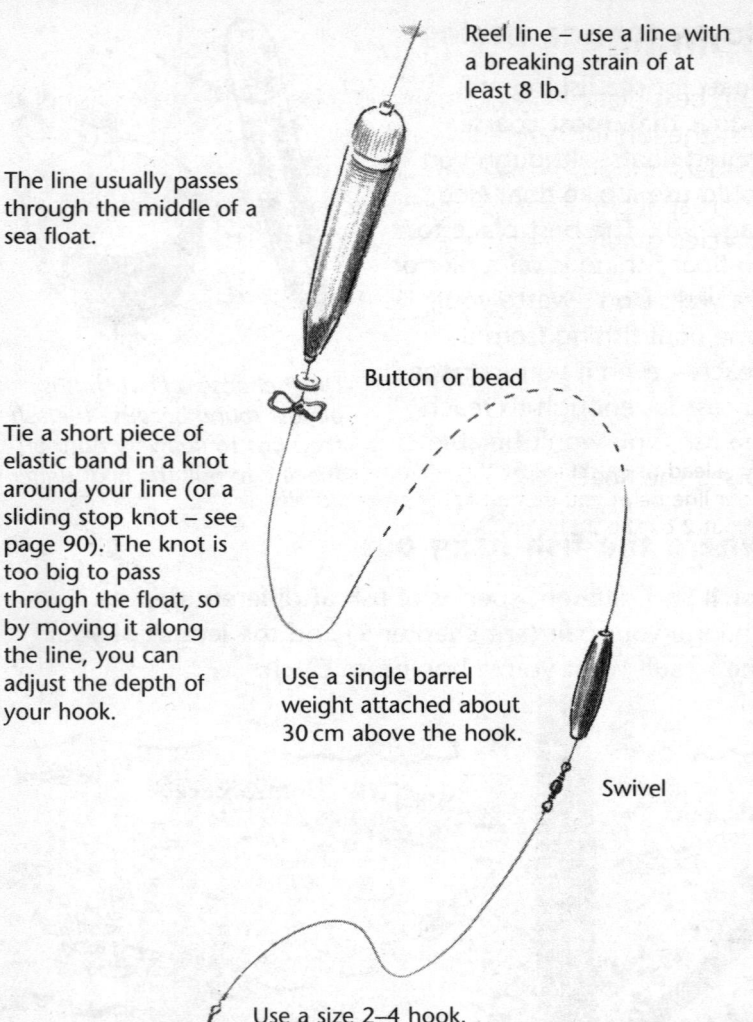

Reel line – use a line with a breaking strain of at least 8 lb.

The line usually passes through the middle of a sea float.

Button or bead

Tie a short piece of elastic band in a knot around your line (or a sliding stop knot – see page 90). The knot is too big to pass through the float, so by moving it along the line, you can adjust the depth of your hook.

Use a single barrel weight attached about 30 cm above the hook.

Swivel

Use a size 2–4 hook.

Tackle tip

Thread a small bead or a shirt button between the float and the rubber band. This will stop the knot getting jammed inside the float.

Spinning

The best place to go spinning is a beach. A small spinner is just the job for catching mackerel. These fish are ferocious feeders and it's possible to catch a huge quantity in a very short space of time. Larger lures can be used for bigger species such as bass.

Reel line – use a line with a breaking strain of 8 lb.

Wye lead or barrel lead – this extra weight on your line helps you cast a light spinner further – about 2 oz should be enough.

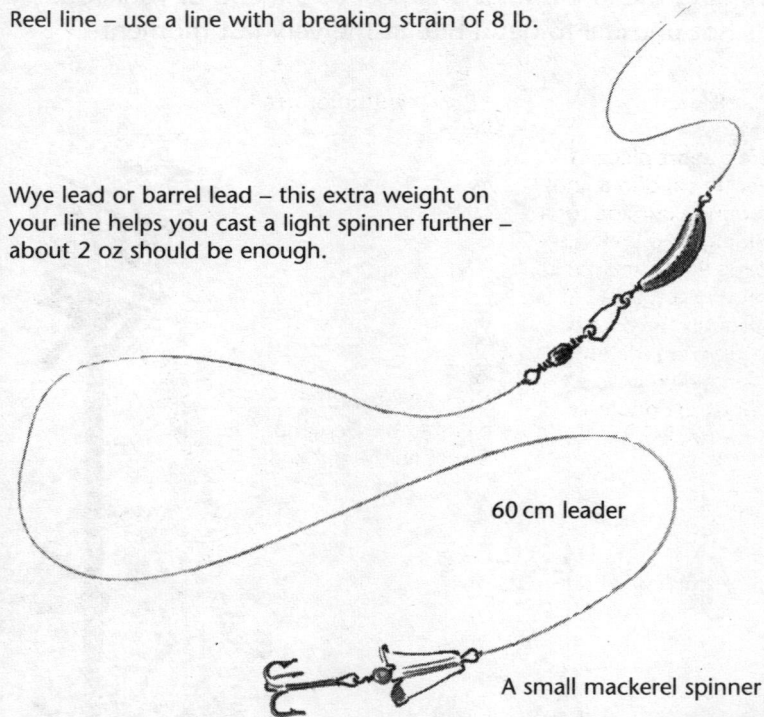

60 cm leader

A small mackerel spinner

Tackle tip

When you get home after a day's sea fishing, always wash the spinners you have used under the tap and allow them to dry before putting them away. This gets rid of the salt that can cause corrosion.

Where to go spinning

Beaches with white water are good places to spin. Cast
beyond the breakers, then work the spinner back through
the surf. The technique is the same as in freshwater
spinning – remember to vary the pace of the retrieve and
twitch the rod from side to side (see page 68). Keep
working the lure until it is almost at the end of your rod.
It's not unusual to get a bite at the very last moment!

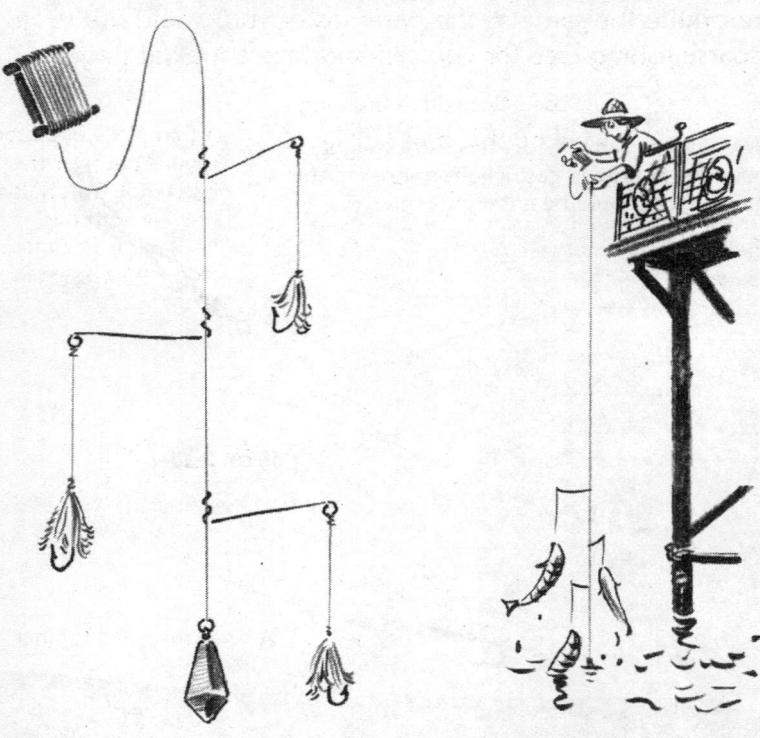

You can't spin off a pier because you are too high above the
water. Use a handline with mackerel feathers instead. Lower
the feathers down into the water, then jig them up and
down. Try fishing at different depths until the bites come.
When you do get a bite, you could end up with three or
four fish on the line at once!

Beachcasting

Fishing in the sea using a ledger is known as beachcasting (or surfcasting). You must have a specialist beachcaster rod for this type of fishing. One of these will cost you at least as much as two CDs but don't forget that you can hire rods quite cheaply from tackle shops too.

The most widely used beachcaster rig is a paternoster. It's not quite the same as the paternoster you would use to go coarse fishing (see for yourself and take a look at page 56).

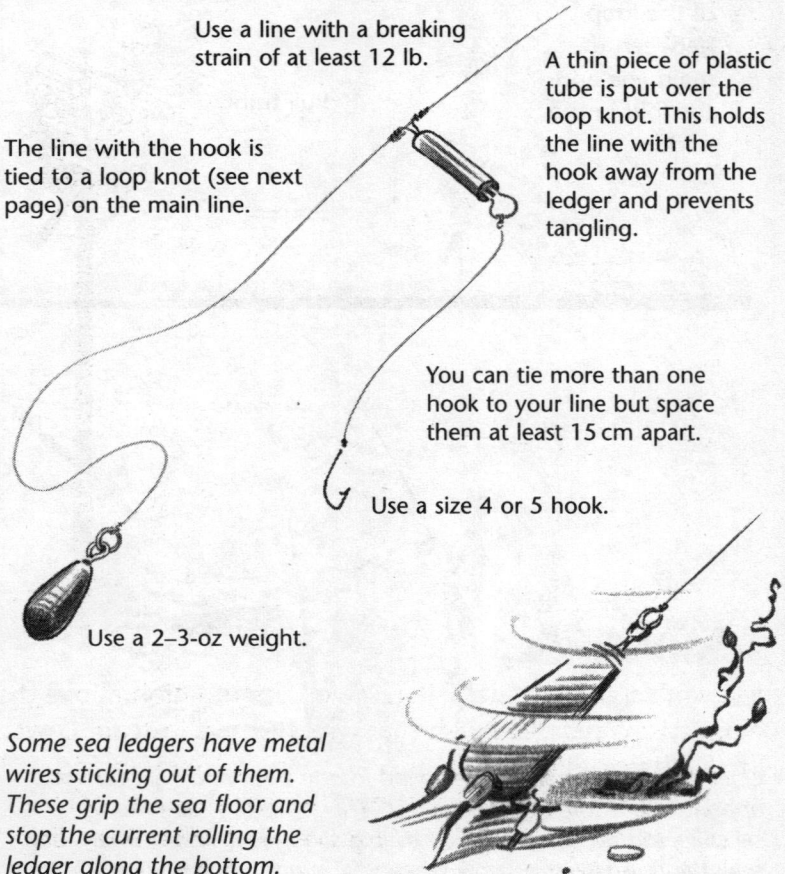

Use a line with a breaking strain of at least 12 lb.

A thin piece of plastic tube is put over the loop knot. This holds the line with the hook away from the ledger and prevents tangling.

The line with the hook is tied to a loop knot (see next page) on the main line.

You can tie more than one hook to your line but space them at least 15 cm apart.

Use a size 4 or 5 hook.

Use a 2–3-oz weight.

Some sea ledgers have metal wires sticking out of them. These grip the sea floor and stop the current rolling the ledger along the bottom.

79

Knot spot

HOW TO TIE A LOOP KNOT

1 Make a loop of main line.

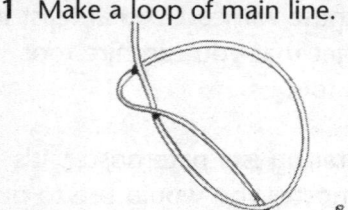

2 Fold the loop over the main line three or four times.

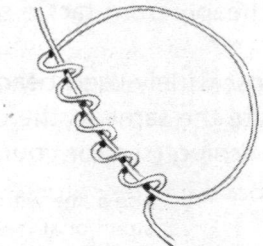

3 Pass the end of the loop between the main line and the fold in the middle.

4 Pull tight.

Once you've cast your ledger, wind in any slack and hold the rod upright or put it in an upright rest. The sea is too rough to use a sensitive rod tip but don't worry – big sea fish pull hard when they take the bait. You will know when you've got a bite all right!

Multiplier reels

A fixed-spool reel is fine for sea fishing, although some anglers prefer to use a kind of reel called a multiplier. On a multiplier reel, the spool spins around when you wind in or release line. Early multipliers were difficult to use because, unless you stopped the spool spinning with your thumb, it spewed out loads of line. The result was a terrible tangle. Modern reels have solved this problem with an in-built magnetic breaking system.

Free spool button – pressing this button allows the spool to spin freely, enabling you to cast.

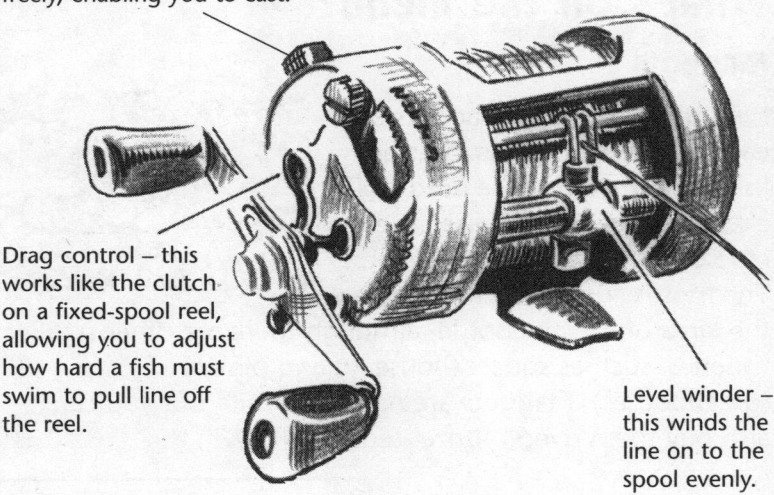

Drag control – this works like the clutch on a fixed-spool reel, allowing you to adjust how hard a fish must swim to pull line off the reel.

Level winder – this winds the line on to the spool evenly.

Record collection

The largest coarse fish ever caught with a rod and line in Britain was a monster carp. It weighed in at just over 55 lb (more than 25 kg).

Rise to the bait

The whole point of ledgering or float fishing is to trick the fish into biting your hook by tempting it with a tasty morsel. There is an enormous variety of baits to choose from, so let's start working our way through the menu!

What's on the menu?

Maggots

Mmmm – delicious! Maggots are easily the most popular coarse-fishing bait and can be used to catch any fish except pike. These little grubs are actually baby flies. The most widely used maggot is the larva of the bluebottle, although there are other smaller varieties, such as squats (housefly) and pinkies (greenbottles). Maggots are naturally white but you can also buy them dyed bronze, red or yellow.

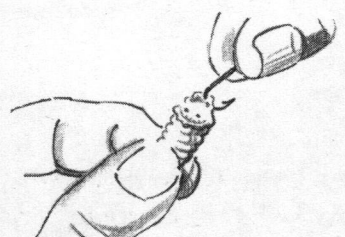

Use a size 16 or 18 hook for a single maggot. Use a size 14 to hook two or three maggots together.

To hook a maggot, pinch it gently between your thumb and forefinger, then push the hook through the flap of skin at the blunt end.

Worms

Worms will catch just about anything that's in the water!
Earthworms (also known as lobworms), redworms and
brandling worms all make excellent bait. You don't need to
buy worms – they are easy to find for free. The best place to
go looking for brandling and redworms is a compost heap.

If it's earthworms you're after, go for a walk on a warm
night, preferably after it's been raining. You'll find them just
lying in the grass. Keep the worms you find in your baitbox
with some damp newspaper.

You can either use a whole worm or just use its tail.

Brandling worms release a yellow liquid when they are
hooked. Although it smells pretty awful to humans, it's great
for attracting fish.

Use a size 14 or 12 hook for worms.

Bread

If worms and maggots seem a bit too wiggly, then use your loaf! Bread is a great bait and can be used in different ways.

Flake

Pull out a soft piece of bread from the middle of the loaf. Push the point of the hook through the flake, then squeeze the bread around the shank (the straight part of the hook) to hold it in place but leave the rest nice and fluffy. It's best to use fresh bread for this – stale bread comes off the hook very easily.

Crust

Cubes of crust are a very popular bait. The tough crust helps keeps the bread

on the hook for longer. Push the hook through the crust and back again.

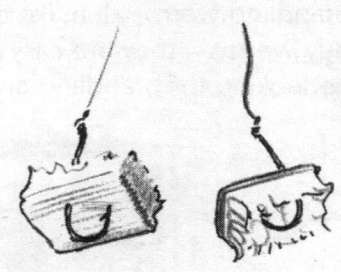

Paste

Soak stale bread in water, then put the mixture in a cloth and squeeze out the excess liquid. You should end up with a firm dough. Adding meat, cheese or even pet food to the paste makes it even more effective.

Use a size 12 hook for bread baits.

Casters

Maggots develop into adult flies inside a pupa called a
caster, just like caterpillars turn into butterflies inside a
chrysalis. These casters make excellent bait. Most anglers
agree that you catch more fish with maggots but bigger
fish with casters.

A caster can be hooked in two ways.

You can nick the hook through the top of the caster...

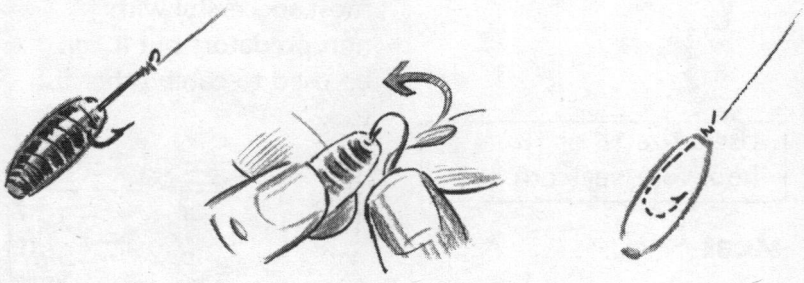

...or you can bury the hook inside the caster.

Use a size 16 or 18 hook for casters.

Sweetcorn

Lots of seeds can be used as bait but sweetcorn is probably the best. It is particularly good for catching tench. You can get tins of corn from your local supermarket. Bait shops sell corn in a wide range of colours and even different flavours (including strawberry!) which prove very popular with the fish. Dried corn is a bit cheaper but you need to soak it in water for 24 hours before you can use it.

Use a size 16 or 18 hook for sweetcorn.

Meat

Luncheon meat, cut into small cubes about 1cm across, is another good bait. You could also try using tinned pet food.

Chub, eels, barbel and carp are particularly fond of meat.

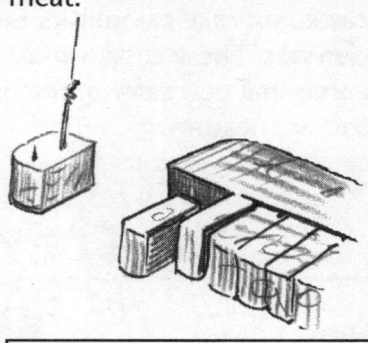

Try a size 12 hook.

Cheese

Any cheese will do for bait but the smellier it is the better. Some cheeses (such as Cheddar) go very hard in cold water so in winter it's best to use soft processed cheese. Cheese is usually most successful with non-predators but it can be used to catch other fish too.

Try a size 14 hook.

Elderberries

You can gather these small
black berries at the end of
summer. They are an
excellent free source of bait
and are particularly good for
catching small species such
as roach and dace.

Use a size 16 or 18 hook.

Hempseed

You can buy these little
round seeds from bait shops
and they are well worth a
try. It's a good idea to throw
a handful of seeds into the
water where you want to
fish a couple of days
beforehand. The fish may
not have seen hempseed
before but once they have
got the taste for it, they
can't get enough!

soak overnight
or boil for 45 mins.

Use a size 16 or 18 hook.

Tackle tip

*Don't put split shot on your line when you are using
elderberries or hempseed – it looks too much like the
bait. Use an olivette instead.*

Pasta

Yes, believe it or not, fish
love pasta! As with
hempseed, when you are
using pasta, it's a good idea
to pre-bait the water to
introduce the bait to the
fish. To prepare the bait,
simply boil the pasta until it
is soft, then allow it to cool.
There's no need to add
tomato sauce!

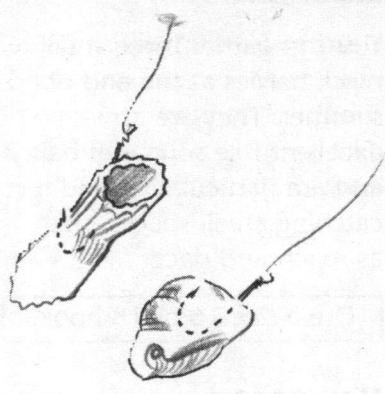

Use a size 14 or 16 hook.

*Pasta is particularly good on
rivers because the shape of the
bait makes it wiggle in the
current and this attracts the fish.*

Also worth trying

All anglers have their favourite deadly bait. Peas, beans,
wheat, barley and even boiled carrots are well worth a go.
Remember, dried foods such as barley or peanuts must be
softened by stewing before they can be used. Place dried
bait in a container and pour boiling water over it, then
leave overnight.

Tackle tip

*Varying your bait and trying something unusual is a
good idea when the fish aren't biting. In waters that are
fished a lot, an unusual bait such as a bit of boiled
carrot might interest a fish that would turn down yet
another maggot.*

Dead bait

Dead bait are small fish (usually bleak or little roach and rudd) that are used to catch pike or zander. They can be 'wobbled' through the water like a spinner or used on a pike float rig. Attach the dead bait to your line using a wire leader with treble hooks.

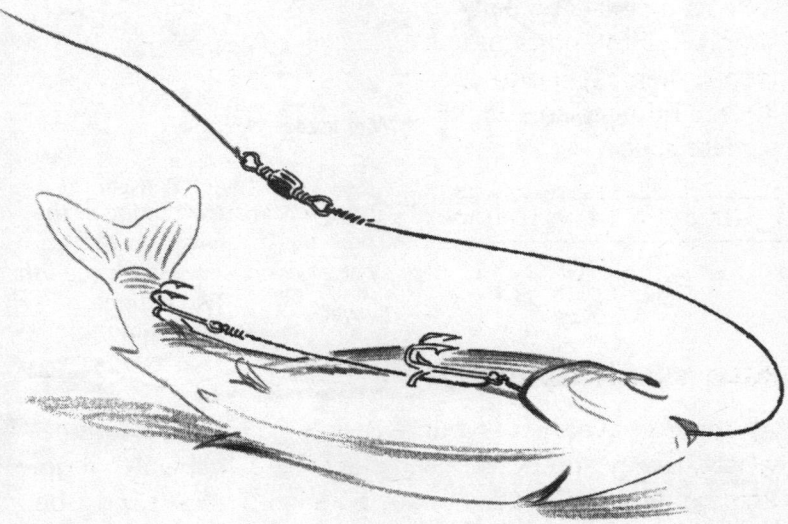

Pass the end of the trace through the gill slit and out of the mouth. Bend the fish's tail so that it wobbles and spins as you pull it through the water, and attach the hooks as shown.

Pike rig

Use a sliding stop knot and a bead to control the distance
between the float and the bait.

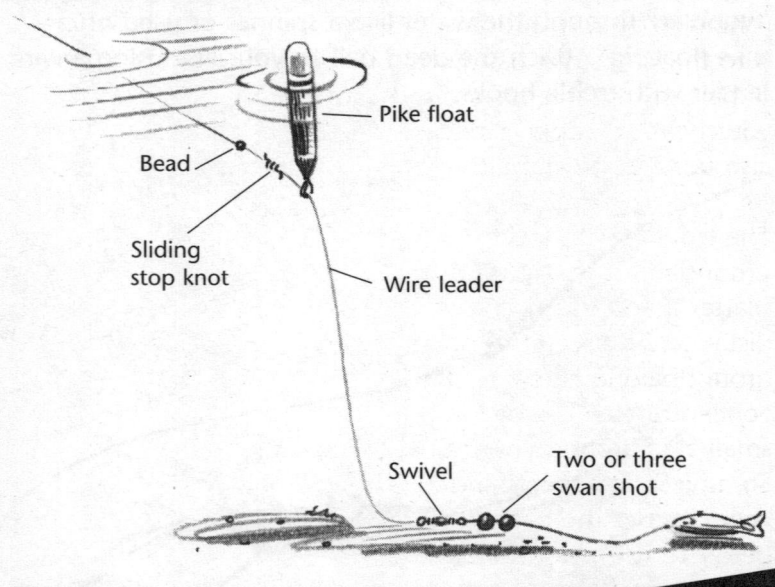

Pike float

Bead

Sliding
stop knot

Wire leader

Swivel

Two or three
swan shot

Knot spot

How to tie a sliding stop knot

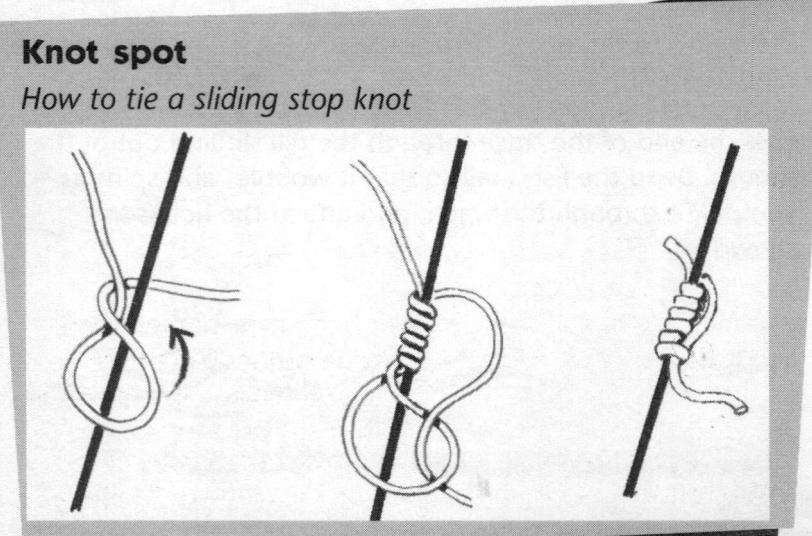

Groundbait

Groundbait is used to attract fish into the area you are fishing. One way of doing this is to throw a small handful of bait so that it lands around your float or ledger. You can also use a bait catapult.

The trouble with loose groundbait is that it tends to scatter if you throw it any distance. The secret of good groundbaiting is to concentrate all the bait in a small area around your hook. So, unless you are fishing very close to the bank, it's better to use a doughball.

Doughball groundbait is made from stale breadcrumbs mixed with water – just like bread paste (see page 84). It's much easier to throw accurately and only breaks up when it hits the water, so all the bait is dropped in one spot. It's a good idea to mix in some of your hook bait (berries, corn, chopped worm or maggots) with the groundbait.

Tackle tip

Don't use too much groundbait, or the fish won't bite the bait on your hook!

Baits for sea fishing

Worms

Worms are very popular sea-fishing baits. The most widely used worms are ragworms and lugworms which live in the salty mud along the coast, but you can also fish with ordinary earthworms. The largest ragworms grow up to 50 cm long. Big worms like these should be chopped up but smaller ones can be hooked whole.

> **BAIT THAT BITES**
> Watch out when handling live ragworms. They have a sharp pair of pincer-like jaws and can give you a painful nip!

Sand eels

Sand eels (also known as lance) can be bought frozen from bait shops. To attach an eel to your line, pass the hook through the jaw and attach it to the stomach.

Limpets

A good supply of bait can be collected for free by using a blunt knife to scrape limpets off the rocks. Pull the limpet out of its shell, then push the hook through its black stomach.

Mackerel

A piece of fresh mackerel is good for catching small fish such as mullet – and other mackerel! Mackerel are cannibals and don't think twice about eating each other. Tying the bait to the top of the hook with a small piece of line will help to keep it on the hook

Crabs

You can buy crabs in bait shops or collect them yourself – try looking under the rocks in rock pools. Crabs that are about the size of a 50p piece are the best.

I've got one!

The moment of truth has arrived. You've got a bite – there's a fish on your line! Don't panic. Stay calm. Once you've read this chapter, you'll know exactly what to do.

How to tell when you've got a bite

Float fishing – your float suddenly ducks under the water.
Ledgering – your swing tip or quiver tip moves.
Spinning – you feel the pull of the fish taking the bait.

Tackle tip

Be prepared – make sure that your reel is ready for action! Before you start fishing, always check that the clutch (see page 18) is set correctly. Put the anti-reverse button on, then try pulling your line. Turn the knob to tighten or loosen the clutch until it is just possible to pull line off the reel. This will stop even a big fish being able to break your line and make a getaway.

The strike

The first thing to do when you get a bite is to strike with the rod. This drives the hook firmly into the fish's mouth. A good strike is very important, otherwise the fish will simply spit your hook out.

How to strike

Strike by lifting the tip of the rod up. The action should be smooth and sharp. Don't flick your rod or give it a massive yank or you will pull the hook out. Maintain a steady pressure on the line – don't let it go slack. Allow the rod to bend gently, using your reel to keep the line taut. With the strike completed and the hook set, you are now ready to play the fish.

95

When is a bite not a bite?

The answer is, when it's a nibble. When you go float fishing
or ledgering you will find that fish often nudge or bump
the bait before they actually make a grab for it. This is
known as a nibble. It will make your float wobble and cause
your swing or quiver tip to tremble. You don't have to
worry about nibbles if you're spinning because predators
attack the bait much more decisively.

Timing your strike

The timing of your strike is critical. If you wait too long, the
fish will gobble the bait and spit out the hook. If you strike
too soon, the hook won't actually be in the fish's mouth
and you won't get the fish on the line. Strike the moment
you get a proper bite but don't strike at a nibble!

Playing the fish

Playing the fish is the most exciting part of fishing. When a
fish is first hooked, it will fight like crazy to escape. That's
when you have to play it, keeping it on the line until it will
allow you to reel it in.

The bigger the fish, the bigger the fight you've got on your
hands. However, as long as you've set your clutch correctly
(see page 18), the fish won't be able to break your line and
escape.

Remember these two golden rules when you are playing a
fish:
• Never point your rod at the fish!
• Always keep the line tight.

It's a fact!

*Fish can swim very fast. An average size fish has a top
speed of about 25 km/h – that's as fast as an Olympic
sprinter!*

I've got one!

Pumping a fish

Don't panic if the fish makes a dash for it. Hold your rod up and keep the pressure on the line but don't try reeling in. Wait until the fish has slowed down, then lower the tip of your rod and quickly wind in the slack. Stop winding when your rod is horizontal and steadily pull the rod up again. This is known as pumping the fish. Keep doing this until the fish is close enough to be landed – or tries to run again!

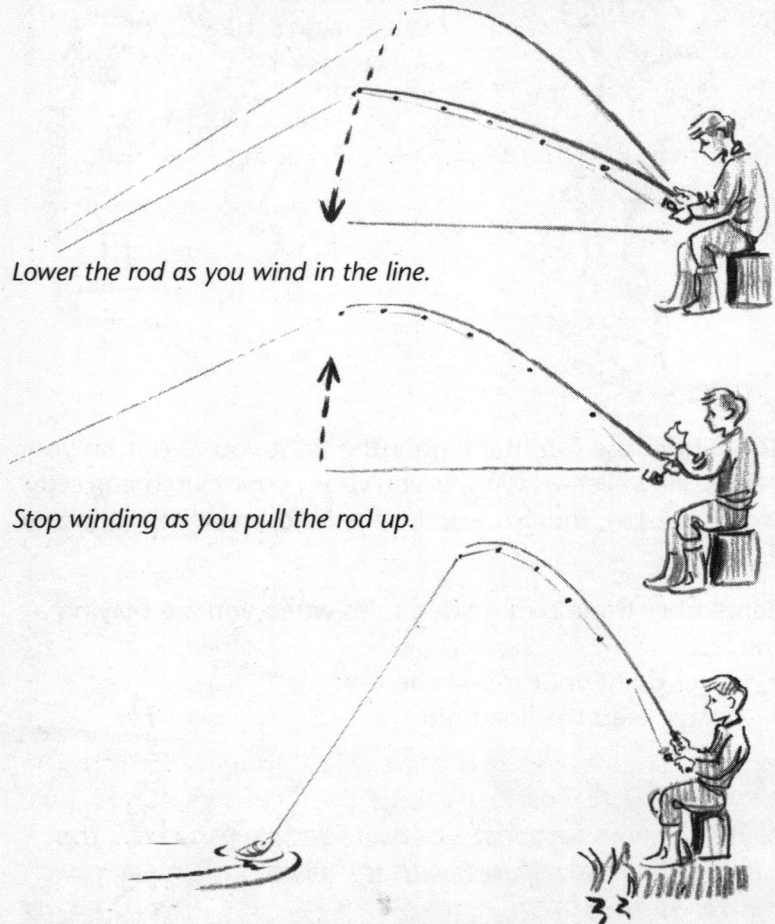

Lower the rod as you wind in the line.

Stop winding as you pull the rod up.

Keep pumping the fish until it is close enough to land.

Turning a fish

If the fish starts swimming towards an underwater obstacle such as a fallen tree or a weed bank, you must make it change direction or your line could end up getting snagged. The way to turn a fish is by applying side strain to the rod.

Lower the rod so that the tip is just above the surface. Point the rod towards where the fish is swimming, then pull hard in the opposite direction. Hang on tight and don't lose your nerve – the fish will be forced to turn!

You can also use this technique to wear out a big fish.

The tip of your rod should be just above the surface as you pull hard away from the fish.

In an emergency, when a powerful fish is refusing to turn and there's a real danger of your line getting snagged, put your finger on the spool as you pull against the fish. This will stop the reel releasing line and give the fish no choice but to change course, although you run the risk of your line breaking.

I've got one!

Landing a fish – coarse fishing

As the fish starts to tire, slip your landing net into the water. Never try to land a fish that is still thrashing around. Wait until it has been played out then draw it over the net.

An exhausted fish lies on its side and can be pulled gently over the net. Keep the net still – bring the fish to the net, not the net to the fish!

As you lift the net out of the water, lower your rod and let the line go slack.

Tackle tip

Before you reach for your landing net, make sure your reel's anti-reverse button (see page 18) is on. This stops the reel spinning backwards when you let go of it and allows you to control the rod with one hand.

Landing a fish – sea fishing

If you are fishing high above the water, from a pier or sea wall, you'll need to use a drop net to land your catch. Lower the net like a basket into the water, then bring the fish above it. Raise the net to stop the fish escaping, put your rod down and haul the net up.

Tackle tip

It's best to keep the drop net in the water so that it is ready when you need it. Dropping a net down in front of a fish will scare it and make it swim away.

When you are fishing from the shore, you don't need a net at all. Just keep reeling in the line until your fish is in the shallows then, with a final pull of your rod, drag your catch ashore on to the shingle or sand.

Handling

Take great care when handling your catch. Never forget that a fish is a living creature and deserves to be treated with respect. So remember these rules:

Always wet your hands before you pick up a fish. Your dry skin can damage the delicate scales on its body.

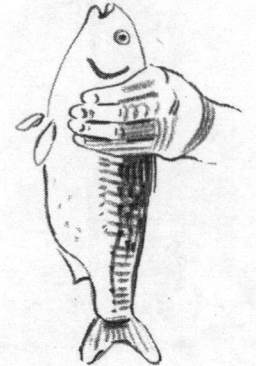

Grip the fish just behind the gills to pick it up. Hold it firmly, otherwise you'll drop it!

Large fish should be wrapped in a wet towel. This stops them flapping about and makes them easier to control. But always make sure the towel is soaking wet before you wrap it around the fish.

Never put a fish on the ground without a wet towel or unhooking mat underneath it. Sharp stones and rough surfaces can cause serious injuries.

Watch out for spines and teeth!

Perch have sharp spines along their dorsal fins, pike have sharp teeth and zander have sharp teeth and spines! It's best to wear a pair of tough gloves when handling these species. But don't forget that the gloves should be wet to avoid hurting the fish.

Removing the hook

The hook should come out of the fish's mouth quite easily.
Grip it by the shank and push back through the hole it
made – it's easy! If the fish is hooked in the lip, you can do
this with your fingers but if the hook is caught inside the
fish's mouth, you'll need a disgorger (see page 36).

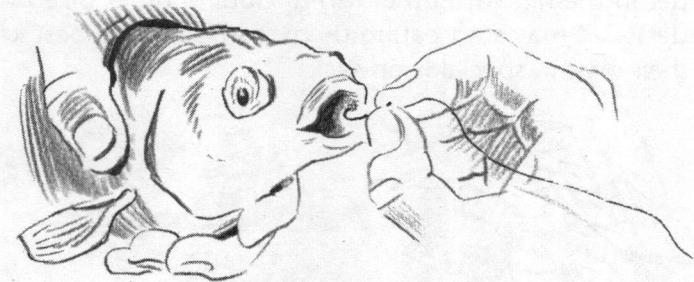

Unhooking a large pike calls for special precautions – and a
pair of forceps! Wrap the fish in a damp towel and sit with
your legs astride it. Slide your finger inside the pike's gill
cover and gently lift its head to open its jaw. If the hook is
caught near the back of its mouth, don't put your fingers in
among all those teeth. Insert the forceps through the gill slit
but take care not to damage the pike's delicate gills.

I've got one!

Keeping and releasing fish

You can keep the fish you catch in a keep-net but only for a short period of time – no more than an hour or so. Always set up your keep-net in a shady spot away from the Sun and make sure at least two-thirds of the net is underwater. Never throw a fish into the net and never put a pike or a zander in the net with other fish (including other pike or zander) as it may start eating them. Large fish are best kept on their own in special keep-sacks.

Unless you are fishing in a competition, keeping the fish you catch is pointless. It's much kinder to return them to the water immediately and let them swim away. Who knows, you might even catch one of them again!

To release a fish, hold it gently underwater between your cupped hands. Support it, keeping it upright, until it is ready to swim away.

 **Fish faces**

M eet the fish you want to catch! Learn how to identify
some of the different species.

Parts of a fish

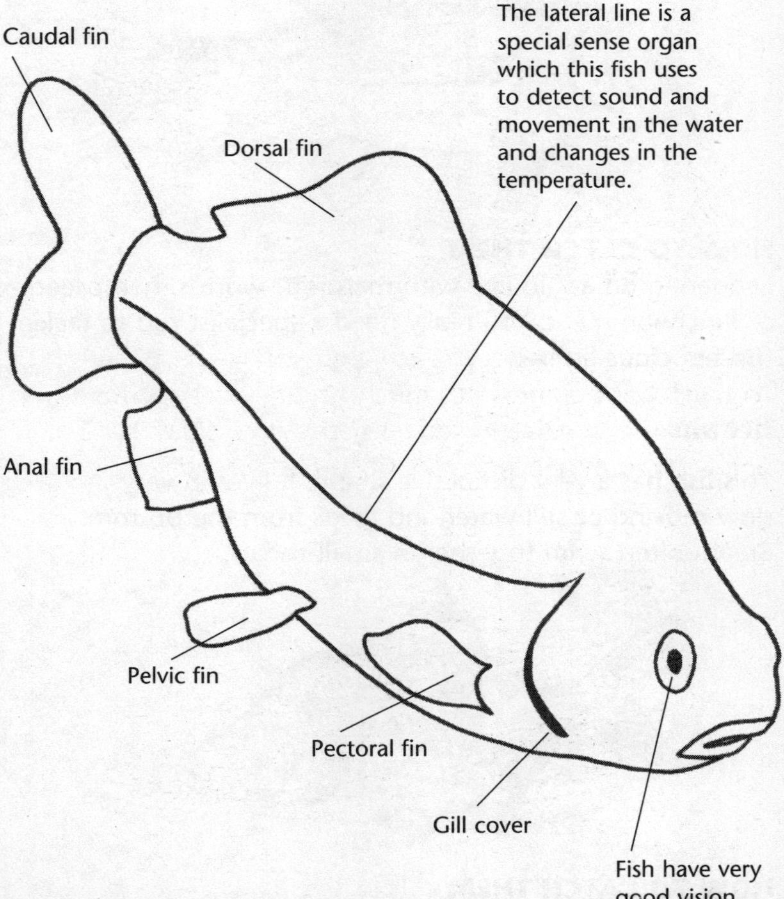

Caudal fin

The lateral line is a
special sense organ
which this fish uses
to detect sound and
movement in the water
and changes in the
temperature.

Dorsal fin

Anal fin

Pelvic fin

Pectoral fin

Gill cover

Fish have very
good vision.

Freshwater fish

Barbel

A very powerful fish, usually found along the bottom of fast-moving, clean water. It has small scales, a long snout and a big mouth with four whiskers called barbels, which is how it got its name.

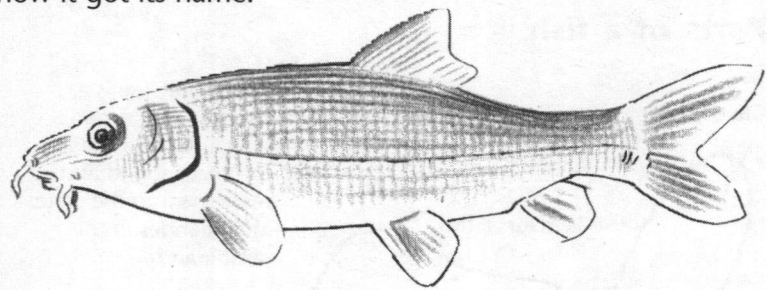

HOW TO CATCH THEM

Ledgering on a 7-lb line with maggots, worms, hempseed or luncheon meat. You really need a specialist rod to tackle this ferocious fighter.

Bream

This fish has a very distinctive shape. It lives in very slow-moving or still water and feeds from the bottom. Bream often swim together in small shoals.

HOW TO CATCH THEM

Ledgering on a 4-lb line with maggots, casters or bread.

Carp

Carp are very powerful fish. There are several different varieties, including the common carp, leather carp, crucian carp and mirror carp. Carp fishing is a specialist skill – this is not a fish for inexperienced anglers!

HOW TO CATCH THEM

Carp fishing requires an 8–10-lb line and a specialist carp rod. The best baits for carp are bread, sweetcorn and worms.

Chub

Chub are usually found in rivers, often in quiet spots near the bank under overhanging trees, or between beds of weed. The fish has a wide, blunt head and a large mouth.

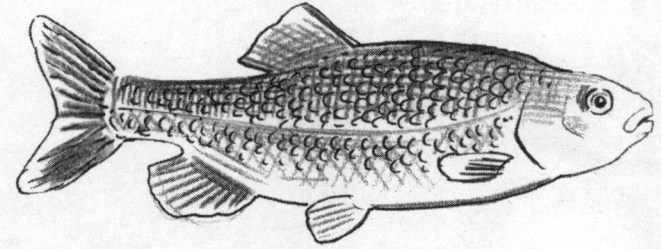

HOW TO CATCH THEM

Ledgering (4–5-lb line) or trotting (2–3-lb line) using casters or maggots.

Dace

Dace are often confused with small chub. The easy way to tell them apart is to look at the anal fin. The chub's anal fin is wider in the middle than at the edges and on a dace it's the other way round. A dace also has a much smaller mouth than a chub.

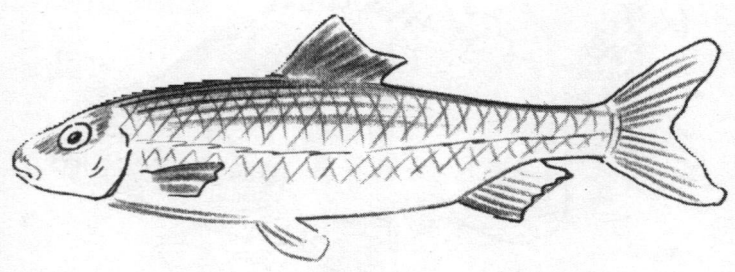

HOW TO CATCH THEM
Trotting with a 2-lb line, using maggots or casters for bait.

Eels

Eels can be a nuisance because they often take a bite out of bait that's intended for something else. However, if you're not too fussy about what you catch, they can be good fun as they put up a great fight.

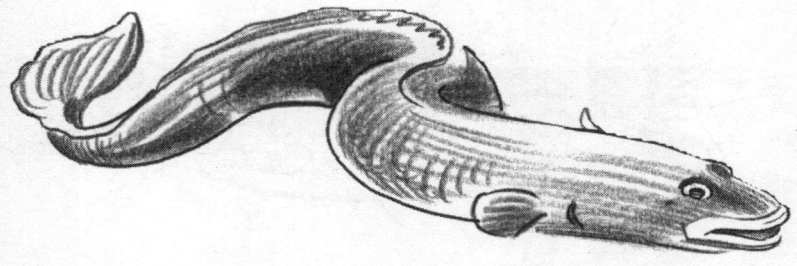

HOW TO CATCH THEM
Ledgering with worms on a 4–5-lb line.

Perch

The striped body and spines of a perch are easy to identify. Perch live in lakes and reservoirs as well as in slow-moving rivers. Small perch live in shoals but larger specimens are usually loners.

HOW TO CATCH THEM

Spinning with a small spoon or spinner on a 5–6-lb line, or ledgering with worms using a slightly lighter line.

Pike

There is no mistaking a pike when you catch one. These fierce fish are shaped like torpedoes and are just as deadly, feeding on other fish, frogs and even ducklings! Pike are found in almost all types of water.

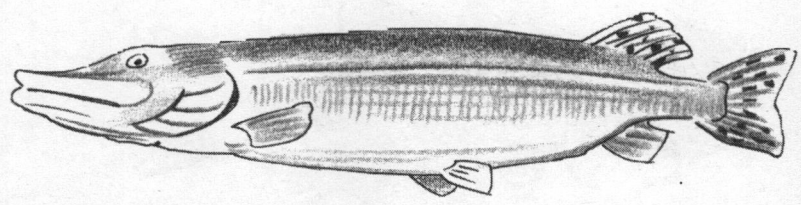

HOW TO CATCH THEM

You really need a specialist rod and a heavy (10–12-lb) line for pike fishing. You can use spinners, plugs or deadbait.

Roach

Roach are the most common freshwater fish, but that doesn't make them any less popular among anglers. They are found in all types of water and usually swim together in large shoals containing up to a hundred fish. Roach have a very visible lateral line. They vary in colour but are usually silvery blue.

HOW TO CATCH THEM

Float fishing (2-lb line) or ledgering (3-lb line) with maggots, casters or bread (especially flake).

Rudd

Rudd are sometimes confused with roach. The colour of their fins should help you tell them apart – rudd have bright orange fins while roach have dull red fins. The pelvic fins on a rudd are in front of its dorsal fin. Rudd are found mainly in still water and usually live close to weeds.

HOW TO CATCH THEM

Float fishing (2-lb line) or ledgering (3-lb line) with maggots, casters or bread.

Tench

Tench are easy to identify. They are a luminous green colour, have very small scales and are covered in a thick layer of slimy mucus. A tench has a small barbel in each corner of its mouth and small red eyes. It feeds on the bottom and is a particularly exciting fish to catch.

HOW TO CATCH THEM

Try using the lift method or ledgering on a 5–6-lb line. The best bait to use is sweetcorn or bread.

Zander

Zander (also known as pikeperch) are usually found in still water. Small zander hunt together in shoals. Larger fish tend to be solitary. A zander has a flat head, spines and razor-sharp teeth.

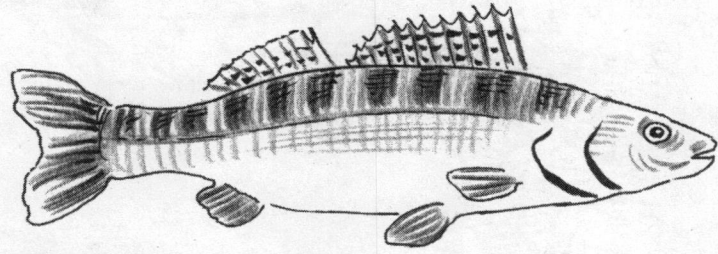

HOW TO CATCH THEM

Try spinning using a 5–6-lb line and a spoon or wobbling deadbait.

111

Fish faces

FISH MAP

Different fish like different types of water. These maps will help you track them down.

Deep fast water
on narrow bends:
barbel

Very shallow, rocky water:
don't bother fishing here

Cool, shadowy
water under
overhanging
branches: rudd,
roach, perch and
chub – a great
fishing spot!

Gently flowing deep
water on wide bends:
chub

Fish faces

Shallow eddies: dace, rudd,
roach, perch and chub

Reeds: pike, rudd and roach

Still water:
rudd and
roach

Lilies: bream and rudd

Deep eddies: pike, perch and zander

Slow water above weir: roach, bream and rudd

Fast water below weir: barbel

Among the branches of a fallen tree: perch and chub

Sea fish

There are many different types of fish in the sea. Here are a few you are most likely to catch.

Bass

Bass have distinctive spines on their front dorsal fin. They are found off the southern coast of the UK. The best time to fish for them is in the summer, when they are usually found nearer the shore. This fish is highly prized by anglers because it is good to eat.

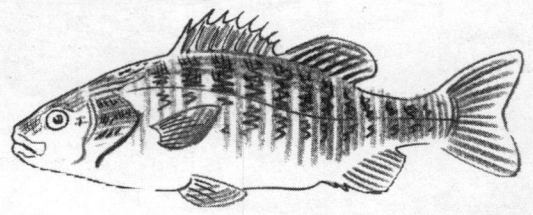

HOW TO CATCH THEM
Casting into the surf with spinners or lures or beachcasting with worms and crabs.

Cod

Cod have three separate dorsal fins and two anal fins. They also have a single barbel that hangs down from the chin. Cod are bottom feeders and are closely related to pollack and haddock. This is another tasty fish to eat.

HOW TO CATCH THEM
Beachcasting, using worms or eels as bait.

Conger

If you're lucky enough to hook a conger, you'll have a really exciting battle on your hands. Once you've beached your catch, however, don't try to remove the hook on your own because conger eels have a ferocious bite – get some help from a more experienced angler!

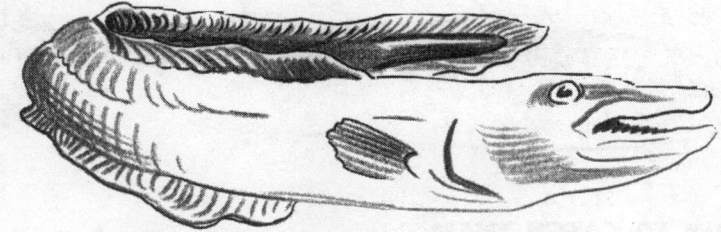

HOW TO CATCH THEM

Beachcasting, using a piece of fish as bait. Conger usually feed at night.

Flatfish

There are lots of different types of flatfish, including plaice, sole and flounder. These fish start out life looking like most other types of fish but as they get older, one eye moves across to the other side of the head and they flip on to their side.

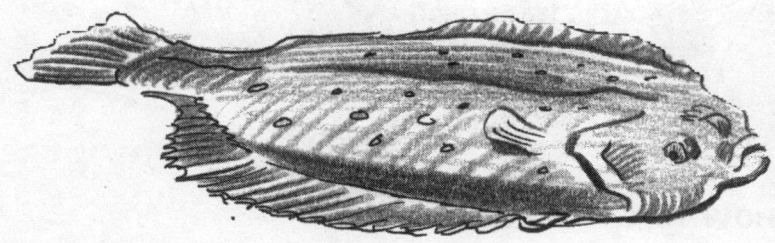

HOW TO CATCH THEM

Beachcasting, using crabs or worms.

Mackerel

Mackerel are very common in the sea. They usually grow about 30 cm long and have a striped skin. They will attack most types of bait and are quite easy to catch in large numbers.

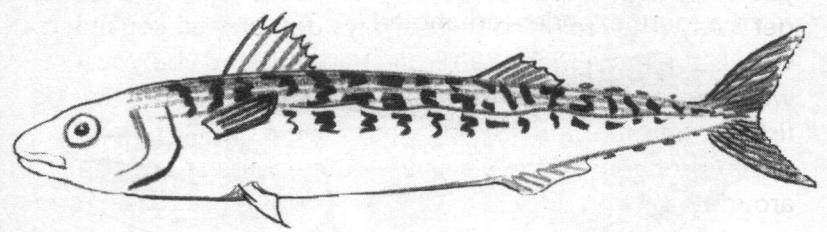

HOW TO CATCH THEM
Spinning with a spinner or jigging mackerel feathers.

Mullet

Mullet is one of the hardest fish to catch and is a real test of your skill. It is usually found in quiet estuaries. A mullet has a long, thin body and a broad head. Mullet are scavengers and will eat almost anything. Some anglers even recommend using banana as bait!

HOW TO CATCH THEM
Float fishing on a light line (5 lb) with bread or worms.

118

In conclusion

Every time you go fishing, you set off on an adventure. Today could be the day you land an absolute whopper – a really huge fish that's so big you can barely hold it up while your pals take a photo. Or maybe an even bigger fish will get away (the *really* big ones always do!) and all you're left with is the memories of a terrific battle. Or maybe you won't get a nibble all afternoon. That's the last time you go fishing there but at least you got to see a big fat heron – which probably also explains why there weren't any fish around!

Fishing is a truly amazing hobby. Everyone can do it. It doesn't matter how old you are, or whether you're a boy or a girl. You may not always catch something – but you should always have a great time. To make sure that you do, just remember these three golden rules.

- Treat the fish you catch with respect and learn how to handle them correctly.
- Always pay attention to safety and follow the rules laid down in this book.
- Leave the spot where you've been fishing as you would hope to find it and take your rubbish home.

Good Luck!

Taking things further

This book can teach you lots about fishing but there is still loads more you can learn. One way to improve your skills is to chat to other fishermen. Don't be afraid to ask for help from other people who are fishing. Anglers are a friendly bunch and are usually very happy to pass on advice and tips.

But the best thing to do is become a member of your local angling club. There are all sorts of advantages to joining a club. Not only are clubs an amazing source of information but they also organise fishing trips, competitions and lessons. To find out about the fishing club nearest you, write to:

The National Federation of Anglers
Halliday House, Eggington Junction, Derby DE65 6GU.
Tel: 01283 734 735

OTHER USEFUL INFORMATION
The National Junior Anglers Association organises competitions and matches for young anglers. It can also help you to find out about your nearest club and may be able to tell you about the good places to fish near where you live. For more information write to:

The National Junior Anglers Association
75 Stoney Rock Lane, Beckett Street, Leeds LS9 7TB.
Tel: 01132 938943

National Fish Week is an annual event. Contact the organisers at the address below to find out what's going on near you. Plenty of the activities and competitions are organised with young anglers in mind. To find out more write to:
National Fish Week
Merly House, Merly House Lane, Wimborne, Dorset BH21 3AA.

Magazines

You'll find lots of fishing magazines on the shelves of your local newsagent. Some are for advanced anglers and deal with specialist subjects such as carp fishing, but there are plenty of others to choose from. Take a look at *Let's Go Fishing*, published by David Hall, for example, which is specifically for young anglers hoping to improve their skills.

Other general fishing magazines include:

Improve your Coarse Fishing
Angler's Mail
Coarse Angling

Websites

There is plenty of fishing information on the Internet – more than 120,000 pages of it, to be precise! You can read all about the exciting adventures of other anglers, learn more about fishing techniques and find out about local clubs and events near you. And remember, you don't need your own computer to surf the Net. More and more libraries are going on-line every month and most allow children to use the computers for free. Here are just a few of the sites you will find in cyberspace.

http://dir.yahoo.com/regional/countries/united_kingdom/recreaction_and_sports/outdoors/fishing/

A directory of useful websites to do with angling in the UK including fishing clubs and magazines.

http://www.fire.org.uk/nfa

The official website of the National Federation of Anglers with news, articles and stacks of information.

Taking things further

http://www.where-to-fish.com/

At this site, you can find the details of more than 3000 places to go fishing in the UK.

http//www.fishing.co.uk

This is the address of a free fishing Internet magazine (or e.zine).

http://www.services-online.co.uk/angling/

Find out where your nearest tackle shop is and the addresses of lots of local places where you can go fishing.

Glossary

anti-reverse button A button on a reel which, when pressed, stops the handle turning backwards, unwinding the line.

Arlesey bomb The traditional type of weight used for ledgering.

Avon A type of float used on rivers. It is named after the River Avon.

bale arm The arm on a fixed-spool reel which winds line around the spool. Closed-face reels have a bale pin instead.

bailiff A person who patrols the bank selling fishing permits and checking rod licences.

balsa A type of float used only on very fast-flowing rivers.

barbed hook A hook with a curved point.

breaking strain Fishing lines come in different strengths known as breaking strains. These tell you how much weight a line can take before it snaps.

bush A bush is used when fishing with a pole to prevent the elastic rubbing against the edge of the pole.

clutch The adjustable knob on a reel which controls how hard a fish must pull before more line is released. Correctly set, the clutch makes it almost impossible for a fish to break your line.

coarse fishing Fishing for freshwater fish (except trout or salmon, which are known as game fish).

disgorger A device for removing hooks.

eye A loop through which line is passed.

fresh water Water that isn't salty.

keep-net A long net used for keeping your catch in. Keep-nets should only be used when you are fishing in a competition.

landing mat A plastic-coated foam mat which the fish is placed on while you remove the hook. Don't forget to make sure that the surface of the mat is nice and wet before you put the fish on it.

ledger A medium or large weight used to carry a baited hook to the bottom. Fishing in this way is called ledgering.

multipliers A type of reel used mainly for spinning and sea fishing.

olivette A long thin weight (usually small) which is mostly used for pole fishing.

peacock The quills of peacock feathers can be used to make floats. Most anglers think peacock floats are best, although they tend to be the most expensive.

permit A fishing permit is a ticket that allows you to fish a particular stretch of water. Some permits are just for a day, but others can last for a whole year.

Glossary

plugs A type of artificial lure. Most plugs are fish-shaped and float until they are retrieved through the water.

plummet A weight used to measure the depth of the water.

pole Like a rod but different! A pole is a long tube. The fishing line is attached to a length of elastic inside the pole.

quiver tip A flexible and sensitive rod tip used for ledgering.

rig Another word for terminal tackle.

rubber A small rubber band that fits over a stick float and attaches it to the line.

rod licence You must have a licence for your rod before you can go coarse fishing if you are 12 years old or more. You can buy a rod licence from a post office.

sarkanas A type of reed which can be used to make very good floats.

shank The straight part of a hook.

shot A small round weight.

spade end The flat end of a hook that does not have an eye.

spinner An artificial lure which spins as it is pulled through the water. Fishing with any type of artificial lure (even one that doesn't spin) is known as spinning.

spool The part of the reel which the line is wound around.

spoon An artificial lure which wobbles as it is pulled through the water.

stick float A type of float used in running water.

strike The action of pulling the rod up to push the hook into the fish's mouth when you get a bite.

stonfo connector This is used when fishing with a pole to connect the elastic to the fishing line.

swan shot Another name for larger shot sizes, particularly SSG.

swim The patch of water you are fishing in is called your swim.

swimfeeder A hollow tube with holes in the sides, filled with bait.

swing tip An extension attached to the end of your rod via a flexible rubber tube. It is used for ledgering on calm water.

terminal tackle The tackle at the end of your line (eg a float, weights and a hook).

trotting A float-fishing technique in which you allow the float to drift downstream on the flow of a river or stream.

waggler A type of float used on still water.

whip Like a pole but without the elastic. The line is tied on to the end of the last section of tubing.

Index

Index

super.activ

All you need to know

0 340 773294	Acting	£3.99	☐
0 340 764686	Athletics	£3.99	☐
0 340 791578	Basketball	£3.99	☐
0 340 791535	Cartooning	£3.99	☐
0 340 791624	Chess	£3.99	☐
0 340 791586	Computers Unlimited	£3.99	☐
0 340 79156X	Cricket	£3.99	☐
0 340 791594	Drawing	£3.99	☐
0 340 791632	Film-making	£3.99	☐
0 340 791675	Fishing	£3.99	☐
0 340 791519	Football	£3.99	☐
0 340 76466X	Golf	£3.99	☐
0 340 778970	Gymnastics	£3.99	☐
0 340 791527	In-line Skating	£3.99	☐
0 340 749504	Karate	£3.99	☐
0 340 791640	The Internet	£3.99	☐
0 340 791683	Memory Workout	£3.99	☐
0 340 736283	Pop Music	£3.99	☐
0 340 791551	Riding	£3.99	☐
0 340 791659	Rugby	£3.99	☐
0 340 791608	Skateboarding	£3.99	☐
0 340 791667	Snowboarding	£3.99	☐
0 340 791616	Swimming	£3.99	☐
0 340 764465	Tennis	£3.99	☐
0 340 773332	Writing	£3.99	☐
0 340 791543	Your Own Website	£3.99	☐

Turn the page to find out how to order these books.

ORDER FORM

Books in the super.activ series are available at your local bookshop, or can be ordered direct from the publisher. A complete list of titles is given on the previous page. Just tick the titles you would like and complete the details below. Prices and availability are subject to change without prior notice.

Please enclose a cheque or postal order made payable to Bookpoint Ltd, and send to: Hodder Children's Books, Cash Sales Dept, Bookpoint, 39 Milton Park, Abingdon, Oxon OX14 4TD. Email address: orders@bookpoint.co.uk.

If you would prefer to pay by credit card, our call centre team would be delighted to take your order by telephone. Our direct line is 01235 400414 (lines open 9.00 am – 6.00 pm, Monday to Saturday; 24-hour message answering service). Alternatively you can send a fax on 01235 400454.

Title .... First name .... Surname ....

Address ....

....

....

Daytime tel .... Postcode....................................

If you would prefer to post a credit card order, please complete the following.

Please debit my Visa/Access/Diner's Card/American Express (delete as applicable) card number:

Signature ....Expiry Date ....

If you would NOT like to receive further information on our products, please tick ☐ .